PREMIUM BEER DRINKER'S GUIDE

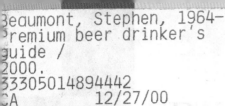
PREMIUM BEER
DRINKER'S GUIDE

STEPHEN BEAUMONT

FIREFLY BOOKS

A FIREFLY BOOK

Published by Firefly Books Ltd. 2000

Copyright © 2000 Denise Schon Books Inc.
Text Copyright © 2000 Stephen Beaumont
A Denise Schon Book

First Printing

Canadian Cataloguing-in-Publication Data

Beaumont, Stephen, 1964 –
    Premium beer drinker's guide: The world's
strongest, boldest and most unusual beers

Includes index.
ISBN 1-55209-510-x

1. Beer.   I. Title

TP577.B417 2000   641.2'3   C00-93048-5

U.S. Cataloging-in-Publication Data

Beaumont, Stephen, 1964 –
    Premium beer drinker's guide : The world's
strongest, boldest and most unusual beers/ Stephen
Beaumont. – 1st ed.
[224] p. : col. ill. ; cm.
Includes index.
ISBN 1-55209-510-x
1. Beer.   I. Title
641.2 / 3 –21   2000   CIP

Published in Canada in 2000 by
Firefly Books Ltd.
3680 Victoria Park Avenue
Willowdale, Ontario
Canada M2H 3K1

Published in the United States in 2000 by
Firefly Books (U.S.) Inc.
P.O. Box 1338, Ellicott Station
Buffalo, New York
USA 14205

Produced by: Denise Schon Books Inc.
Design: Counterpunch/Linda Gustafson
Editorial: Jennifer Glossop
Index: Barbara Schon

Printed and bound in China

*The Publisher acknowledges the financial support of the Government of Canada through
the Book Publishing Industry Development Program for its publishing activities.*

PHOTO CREDITS

Hal Roth: pp. 45, 61, 75, 85, 99, 113, 132, 145, 163, 179
We thank the following people and organizations for sharing their images:
Stephen Beaumont: pp. 13, 15, 193, 212–213; Belgian National Tourist Office: pp. 2, 10–11, 22, 35, 55, 127, 159; British
    Tourist Authority: pp. 42–43, 108, 122, 188, 153, 168; German National Tourist Office: pp. 65, 90, 198–199;
    Ommegang Brewery: 24–25, 28.
Photographs of beer bottles are either courtesy the breweries or from Hal Roth.

Dedicated to the armies of men and women who make the world's bars, bistros, pubs and cafés work. It is all well and good to have a great beer at your disposal, but without a comfortable, sociable locale in which to enjoy it with friends, family and neighbors, its pleasures are greatly diminished. Thank you all for your dedicated and much-underappreciated work.

CONTENTS

Few people are ambivalent about beer. Folks love it or hate it; think it is the nectar of the gods or a sadly bitter brew; view it as an honorable and noble beverage or simply as fuel for barroom brawls. Some wage arguments over which brand is better or how a certain style of beer should taste, while others dismiss the whole matter with a wave of the hand and a scornful, "I don't like beer." Passion and beer, it would appear, go hand-in-hand.

Sometimes, however, we let our passions get the better of us. Confronted by an ever-expanding list of beers, we often close our minds to the new possibilities and turn instead to the tried-and-true brand that fits us as comfortably as an old sweatshirt. Still, forever lurking behind that safe decision is a nagging doubt: What if that other beer really is better?

The purpose of this book is to help you deal with that doubt and to encourage you to eschew the safety of the familiar and try that other beer – not always, certainly, but from time to time or on special occasions. Because as rewarding as any familiar brand or style might be, there will always be some situation or circumstance in which another beer will reward you just that much more. The trick is to find the right beer and the right occasion and put them together.

This book is not about beer snobbery, but about beer choice. Thanks to generations of innovative, dedicated brewers, we have glorious choices to enjoy. It would be tantamount to sacrilege to waste them.

Enjoy!

In the more than a decade that I have been writing about beer, I have had the honor and privilege of sharing a pint and a conversation with many of the fine men and women involved in the brewing business. They are the brewers, importers, brewery presidents, sales representatives and, above all else, fellow beer aficionados who make this industry work. To them, and to all the others I will no doubt meet in the future, thank you for making my job one of the most interesting and pleasurable I can imagine.

Thanks also to all those beer lovers around the world who have taken time from their busy schedules to show me around and introduce me to the beers and breweries of their regions. Without your assistance, my road to beer would no doubt have been a much longer and more winding one.

My many editors also deserve my appreciation for affording me the opportunity to spread the word about good beer and for allowing me to make a decent living doing so. In particular, I'd like to thank Tom Dalldorf of *The Celebrator*, John Hansell of *The Malt Advocate*, George Rivers of the now defunct *BarleyCorn*, Anthony Giglio, formerly of *Beer Connoisseur* and *P.O.V.*, Colman Andrews of *Saveur*, Randy Johnson of *Hemispheres*, Beppi Crossariol of *The Globe and Mail* and everybody at the Internet's Real Beer Page. And while I'm on the subject of publishing, thank you to Denise Schon, who signed me to my first book contract and helped bring this most recent one to fruition.

Finally, to my family, friends and, most of all, my lovely and immensely talented wife, Christine, thank you for supporting me, encouraging me and suffering through my endless diatribes about beer.

An Introduction to Premium Beer

Premium Beer Defined

When I began drinking beer in the 1970s, the hierarchy of North American brews was pretty simple: there were regular beers and premium beers. The regular ones were those major-brewery products that we drank on a day-to-day basis, while the premium brands were the slightly more alcoholic offerings from those same breweries, the ones we ordered when we felt like going out on a limb. Imports were as scarce as well-hopped ales; and save for one or two offerings from the better regional breweries, craft-brewed beers were virtually nonexistent.

Immediately following the start of the craft-brewing renaissance – that wonderful period in the mid-1980s when a wave of small breweries sprang up, producing small-batch beers full of flavor and replete with character – things did change but only slightly. Pretty much abandoning the premium beer segment to this new wave of microbreweries, the majors continued to fight for the ordinary beer market among themselves. Meanwhile, the trickle of imported brews slowly built itself up into a steady stream.

Today, the face of the beer market on the North American continent bears little resemblance to that of my earliest days as a beer enthusiast. Brands once thought of as ordinary have been reclassified as premium; those once viewed as premium have become known as superpremium or extrapremium; low-cost brews have flooded the market, putting price pressure on the beers of other categories; what we knew as microbrewery beers are now called craft-brewed beers and range dramatically in quality, style and price; and that steady stream of imports has become a raging torrent. It's no wonder that for many, beer shopping has become as intimidating a prospect as wine buying or car shopping.

Which is wrong. As complex and distinguished a drink as it may be, beer has never been a pretentious beverage. Relaxing, sociable and flavorful, yes; pompous, elitist and incomprehensible, never. Beer has always been class *uncon*scious, the drink of princes and paupers alike, enjoyed as much by the pharaohs of ancient Egypt as by the laborers of pre-Industrial England. It is for after work in Japan and for breakfast in Germany; for warming bones chilled by winter in Sweden and for slaking thirsts brought on by the midday sun in Australia; for celebrations with friends in America and for relaxing with the family in Belgium. In short, beer is the everyday drink for the everyday person.

And premium beer, true premium beer, is the special-occasion drink for those same everyday people. That is the only useful definition of a "premium" beer and the only one that matters. It applies equally to a domestic beer, an import or the product of a brewpub and that of a megabrewing corporation. A premium beer is a special kind of beer that offers you an experience well beyond what you expect out of drinking a beer. Period.

These are the beers that you will find in this book: special beers, ones that stimulate your senses and challenge your perceptions and, above all else, make a bold statement in your glass. Premium beers are not the ones that finance brewing conglomerates or whose names trip easily off the tongues of beer drinkers around the world, but they are the ones that can and often do make a brewery's reputation. They are also the beers that brewers create for the love of the art of brewing, and the ones that we drink because we appreciate that art and will go out of our way to taste its excellence.

There is nothing wrong with a well-made pilsner or a terrifically flavorful amber ale, but those beers will not be mentioned on the following pages because, as good as they are, they are our ordinary, everyday beers. The styles and brands that you will meet in this book are the crème de la crème of the brewing industry worldwide, those beers that either speak to a proud history of brewing or are representative of the modern brewer's creativity at its best. They are the big beers: big in flavor, big in character, big in intensity and frequently big in alcohol. You could call them super-extra-premium or the premier grand crus of the beer world, but I prefer to just call them what they are: truly premium beers.

At its most elemental, beer making is a simple process. In much the same way that wine is in essence just crushed and fermented grapes, beer is simply partially germinated grain that has been steeped in water and then boiled, seasoned and fermented. You could actually make it with only a large pot, a couple of pounds of grain and some water. The result would most certainly be beer; it just might not be beer that anyone would want to drink.

To make a beer people will happily pay money for is a little more difficult. Ingredients must be carefully selected, quantities painstakingly thought out and measured, the length of time and temperature at which the unfermented brew is boiled minutely controlled, and every conceivable variable or hitch anticipated and corrected. For a commercial brewery pumping out thousands, tens of thousands or even millions of barrels of beer, the process can get extremely complicated.

To begin with, there is the most basic and plentiful ingredient – water. Although finding water might seem simple enough, even fresh, pure spring water may not necessarily be suited to brewing. Characteristics such as mineral content and alkalinity (pH level) could make the water wrong for the style of beer being brewed. Adjustments may have to be made, minerals added or filtered out, and even the way the water will react with the other brewing ingredients factored into the equation.

If water is the base upon which a beer is built, then barley malt is the construction material. Malt is made by soaking the barley until germination begins and then kilning the sprouted kernels to bring this growth to a halt. This process releases the barley's starches and readies them for brewing, but further kilning or roasting may be used to add color, flavor and aroma to the grain. In any given beer, the brewer may use a combination of malts ranging from pale bronze to caramel to deep chocolate in color, with each contributing its own unique characteristics to the finished brew.

Once the water has been selected and adjusted, and the barley malt chosen, the two are combined in a vessel known as a mash tun and left to steep at about 65°C (150°F). This process is known as mashing in, its purpose being to convert the grain's starches into fermentable sugars and release them into the water. The resulting sugar water is known as wort.

The third basic beer ingredient is hops. The flowers of a voracious vine known as the wolf plant, or *Humulus lupulus*, hops entered the brewing process as a preservative sometime around 800 to 900 AD. Today, they are employed more for their flavor, aroma and bittering qualities than for their preserving prowess. Always vital to the overall character of a beer, hops virtually define the nature of certain beer styles; for example, the North American pale ale, India pale ale and, to a lesser degree, cask-conditioned best bitter.

Dozens upon dozens of varieties of hops are cultivated around the globe, with more strains being developed all the time. It is in hops that the parallels to grapes grown for winemaking are the strongest, as each hop genus is as individual and distinct as is any wine grape. And like grapes, hops are affected by the soil, climate and circumstances in which they were grown. Thus, a Goldings hop cultivated in its indigenous region of Kent, England, will provide a beer with different qualities than would a Goldings grown elsewhere.

Hops are added to the beer-to-be in the brewkettle after the mash, as the wort is boiling. Typically, this stage – the boil – can last from one to three hours (one-and-a-half to two hours is typical) and anywhere from one to five or more varieties of hops may be added during its progress. Hops added near the start of the boil will contribute more bitterness and flavor to a beer, while those added near the end will contribute more aromatics. The choice of hops and the timing of their additions are vital to the character of the finished beer.

Finally, after the mash and the boil comes the fermentation, the transformation of sugars into alcohol and carbon dioxide. This process is accomplished by the addition of yeast, but the brewer's choice of which of the hundreds of strains of brewer's yeasts to use will profoundly affect the final result. If a bottom-fermenting lager yeast is used, for example, cooler fermentation temperatures and a longer post-fermentation conditioning period will be needed, and a crisper, cleaner beer will result. On the other hand, if a top-fermenting ale yeast is employed, the requirements would include warmer fermenting temperatures and less conditioning time, and the end beer would be rounder and fruitier. And within these two broadly defined families, there is a host of varieties from which to choose: vigorous yeasts; estery (fruity) yeasts; sulfury yeasts; slow-working, almost lethargic yeasts.

Once the yeast has worked its magic, there are more choices to be made. Should the beer be dry-hopped, a process whereby more hops are added to the already-fermented beer in order to heighten the hop aroma and flavor? Will natural carbonation suffice, or should the beer be injected with extra carbon dioxide? How long should it be aged? Is a refermentation in the bottle, known as bottle-conditioning, an option? Pasteurization or filtration? The decision-making process does not stop until the customer is drinking the beer.

Large breweries seeking to maximize their operational efficiency modify the process in two very important ways. First, they make use of inexpensive sources of fermentable sugars, known as brewing adjuncts. In extreme cases, these adjuncts can be simple sugar syrups, but more often they are foods such as rice or corn. (The best-selling beer in the world, Anheuser-Busch's Budweiser, boasts its rice content on the label.) Employed in small amounts of 5% or less of the total mash, adjuncts have little effect upon the finished beer. When used in large quantities, however, adjuncts tend to sweeten a beer and thin its body, particularly when the beer is a lager.

The second big-brewery trick is a process known as high-gravity brewing. The brewer intentionally creates a beer of significantly higher strength than the final brew – say 7.5% alcohol for a beer that will eventually be sold at 5% alcohol. When it comes time to package the beer, the stronger brew is watered down until it reaches the desired alcohol content, which in our example would involve adding five extra gallons of water for every 10 gallons of high-gravity beer. This process is followed to a greater or lesser degree by most major breweries.

The beer-making process as described to this point will create a service-able, possibly very good, potentially outstanding beer. For the purposes of this book, however, it would be unlikely to merit the modifier of "premium." To brew a true premium beer requires a little extra – extra time, extra care, extra effort and, as often as not, extra ingredients. To make a premium beer is to craft something special, a beer that sets the palate to rapturous contemplation and the imagination to soaring. These are the beers on which brewers hang their reputations and the ones that they hold nearest and dearest to their hearts. For the beer aficionado, they are the ne plus ultra.

What the creation of a premium beer most often entails is a significant addition to the amounts of one or more of the basic brewing necessities. This might mean a two-fold increase in hops, with a proportional boost in malt so that the balance does not fall out of the beer, or a major augmentation to the pounds of malt used, if a big-bodied, high-alcohol beer is the goal. Sometimes a new ingredient, such as spice or fruit or another grain, is added or an existing ingredient is altered, as when malt is smoked for a rauchbier.

Regardless of what needs to be done, you can be sure that it will require extra time, expense and effort from the brewer and the brewery. It will all be thought worthwhile, though, because a great premium beer is the stuff on which reputations are made and sales of more ordinary beers are hinged. And although the brewer might occasionally resent the sweat and toil that goes into the creation of the premium brands, in the long run it is labor happily done to achieve a result that stretches the boundaries of brewing creativity.

After all, brewers are not just creators of great beers, they are also beer aficionados and beer consumers. And every bit as much as you or I, they appreciate the intense color, fragrant aromas and complex flavors of a good beer.

THE MYTH OF THE REINHEITSGEBOT

The Bavarian Purity Law of 1516, also known as the Reinheitsgebot, is one of the most popular terms of the modern craft-brewing renaissance. As its name suggests, it is the German act that limits the ingredients allowed in brewing to water, yeast, hops and malt. And judging from the literature disseminated by the marketing departments of hundreds of craft breweries, it is pretty popular in North America, too. But does the Reinheitsgebot mean good beer?

The answer is yes and no. In bottom-fermentation, where purity and cleanliness and an unadulterated supply of ingredients are of paramount importance, the Reinheitsgebot has its place. Since lagers tend to be crisper and cleaner in taste, the use of extra or substitute ingredients tends to affect the flavor of the beer more directly and detrimentally. In lager brewing, then, the Reinheitsgebot makes all sorts of sense.

In top-fermentation, however, the situation is significantly different. Here, richer and more complicated flavors can absorb extra ingredients – indeed even benefit from them – and when judiciously employed, adjuncts such as sugars, spices and fruits can reward an ale with increased character and body. With all the fruity esters and various other flavors already common to top-fermented beer, there is simply more leeway than that allowed in lager brewing.

So, yes, seeing that the brewery proudly endorses the Reinheitsgebot on their label does guarantee you purity in your beer, but it does not say anything about how good it will taste.

DOMESTIC VS. IMPORTED:
THE TRUTH ABOUT PREMIUM BEER

Since the beginning of the North American craft-brewing renaissance, much has been made about the freshness of beer. You could even say that it has been the battleground upon which many of the fiercest marketing wars of the past decade have been waged.

Large breweries now trumpet the "Born on" dates on their labels. These dates tell you not when the beer was brewed or when it finished fermentation, but when it was put in the bottle. Other national brewers, some medium-sized regionals and many small, localized operations list "Best Before" dates on their labels. These dates let you know how long the brewery poo-bahs think that their beer will last – under perfect conditions, of course. And brewpubs make hay of the fact that their customers have the privilege of drinking right alongside the kettles and tanks in which the beer in their glasses was brewed and fermented, regardless of how long it might have spent in the brewery or in a keg prior to being poured.

Through all of this, of course, is the insinuation that the fresher beer is, the better it tastes, and by extension that domestic beer is better than imported beer. (This latter theory is sometimes spelled out in vivid detail by overzealous brewery marketers.) The final conclusion to this rather spurious reasoning would appear to be that, regardless of the ability of the brewer or the style of the brew, the best beer is that which is brewed closest to home.

Alas, this theory makes about as much sense as the idea that homemade wine will beat first-growth Bordeaux every time because it is fresher, or that the best source of water is always going to be the one closest to your home!

It is true that for some beer styles, including virtually all mass-produced lagers, fresher is better. But it is not just time that does a disservice to beer, and it is not every style of beer that will be affected by its passage. Bad storage, for example, is the leading cause of the ruination of beer, and it matters not whether a poorly shelved bottle of beer comes from a brewery around the

corner or on the other side of the world. Light, heat and foul odors are the enemies of all beer, regardless of style, and if any beer is exposed to one or more of these elements over a prolonged period of time, its taste will be ruined. For this reason, the most important factor in deciding where you want to buy your beer is the retailer's ability to keep its stock in tip-top form.

Due to their low levels of protective elements, ales and lagers that are light in color and alcohol are among the worst at tolerating time, so freshness should be considered when purchasing them. Look for bottling or "Born on" dates on the label or case and try to find beer not more than three to four months old, or ask the store proprietor how long the beer has been in stock. These factors are important when buying all light ales and lagers, but more so for the typically lightly hopped beers of a country like Mexico than for more heavily hopped lagers from places like Germany and the Czech Republic. They are particularly important when the beer is packaged in clear or green glass.

On the flip side of the elements that are detrimental to beer are those characteristics that protect it from deterioration. Bottle-conditioning, which involves a final fermentation within the capped or corked bottle, plus high alcohol levels and high hopping rates are all traits that help a beer to weather the passage of time. Additionally, heavier-bodied brews are less likely to be affected by light, heat and odors than are lighter-bodied beers, and a dark-colored or opaque bottle will help protect the beer just that much more. When any or all of these characteristics are present in a beer, the odds of its lasting longer periods of time without ill effect are increased exponentially.

Further, certain classic styles and brands of beer actually benefit from the passage of time. I have sampled beautifully aged beers of five years (a superb Kulmbacher Reichelbräu Eisbock), 17 years (a remarkably developed Cantillon Gueuze) and even 26 years (a richly complex Thomas Hardy's Ale). Stored under proper conditions, there is no reason that these beers and others like them cannot mature and evolve most deliciously.

So how does all of this figure into the question of domestic versus imported premium beers? Simply, save for styles like cask ales, some wheat beers and certain fruit-flavored or spiced brews, the place of origin of the beer has little relevance. If it has been well handled in transit and well stored at the retail level, a premium beer brewed halfway around the world can be every bit as worthy as the one produced across the street. In fact, even cask ales, the most temperamental of all premium beers, can easily survive travel if they are expertly and carefully treated en route. What counts in the long run are the flavor, character and integrity of the beer, not its birthplace.

So the next time someone tells you that any domestic beer is better than the imports, ask him how often he has heard of a domestic brewery producing a gueuze or Trappist ale. And then tell him about the 26-year-old Thomas Hardy's.

Back in the pre-craft-brewing renaissance days of the 1970s and early 1980s, beer had one role and one role only: as a cold, wet, moderately alcoholic beverage. Back then no one spoke of beer as a nightcap or as a satisfying restorative, and on the rare occasion that beer was mentioned in conjunction with food, it was always paired with a hotdog, burger or pizza. Certainly no one would have thought to bring a beer to an elegant dinner.

And there was a very good reason for this. At the time when "premium beer" meant a higher alcohol content and perhaps less corn or rice added to the barley malt, the North American beer market totally lacked a variety of beer styles and flavors. True, different beer labels were available in abundance – the handful of breweries that dominated the market had a veritable bounty of brands on offer – but all of them tasted more or less the same. As beer drinkers, we were like prisoners served the same gruel day after day, content with the tedium of our daily fare because we were oblivious to the scope of flavors found in the rest of the world.

Thankfully, all that has changed. Now we know that beer can be cold and quenching or rich and satisfying; that it is both beverage and food, packed with the nutritive qualities we normally look for in our breakfast cereals; that it comes in an incredible range of hues, from shimmering pale gold to warm mahogany to midnight black; and that it can offer flavors and aromas ranging from sour cherry to toasted walnut and spice cake to iced latte. Thanks to the hundreds of brewers and importers who have expanded our beer selection exponentially over the years, we are beginning to realize that this fabulous drink that we once took so much for granted is one of the world's most diverse and rewarding beverages.

Yet even knowing this, we still tend to sell beer short at the table. We may understand that ale or lager can be as comfortable at a black-tie affair as at the ballpark, but we tend to cling to our habits of hotdogs, burgers and pizza as foods for beer. In the dining room, at the restaurant, around the kitchen table and pretty much everywhere except the backyard patio, wine remains king, with coffee and liqueurs in supporting roles. A beer may make it as a before-dinner drink, but when the time comes to be seated for the meal, the beer glasses are quickly banished. Yet as much as the ale and lager are undeserving of such gustatory prejudice, the premium beer is even more greatly maligned by these misconceptions. Because for certain specific gastronomic needs, absolutely nothing beats a good premium beer.

Scenario 1: The month is June and you are hosting your first dinner party of the summer. To make it special, you add some mesquite chips to the barbecue coals and smoke a pork loin over the aromatic embers. And to drink? A fruity pinot noir would be nice with plain barbecued pork, but it might well be lost beneath the smokiness of this dish. Instead, you fill your guests' glasses with a smoked malt rauchbier from Germany and watch with delight as their eyes widen in amazement at how perfectly the two flavors mesh and complement each other. In one deft move, you have created a party that will not soon be forgotten.

Scenario 2: You have slaved for hours melting chocolate, beating eggs and mixing batter for a dense, sinfully rich and delicious dark chocolate cake. But even the complex sweetness of a sauterne or ice wine risks being overpowered by such potent flavors, and anyway, such wines are far too pricy to submit to that kind of a chancy situation. So you turn to a dark, luxurious, silky smooth Imperial stout as the sweetly perfect partner for your chocolate creation and find that certain beers really do pair divinely with chocolate.

Scenario 3: Spiciness is on the menu with a potful of chicken vindaloo simmering on the stove, and for those who like the pain and pleasure that comes with its use, a bottle of hot sauce awaits at the table. No matter how acidic it may be, though, any wine would be destroyed by this combination, and cold water or iced lager will numb the palate and destroy your guests' ability to taste the wonderful flavors that go along with this peppery heat. So an India pale ale is pulled from the cellar and poured as an accompaniment, with its heavy bitterness calming the spice and its malty backbone providing flavors that sparkle alongside the curry. And a little more pleasure is added to the pain.

The list of scenarios could go on and on: abbey-style ales with beef stews, hefeweizens with salads, cask-conditioned best bitter with a steak and kidney pie, barley wine with chocolate truffles. The important point is that while no premium beer can be all things to all dishes, many are ideally suited to specific foods. They are not simply alternatives to serving wine or spirits, they are better complements.

So take beer with you to the table. Take it to an ordinary meal and make the meal extraordinary; take it to a special occasion and make the occasion that much more memorable; and take it to a friend's table and introduce your friend to the delicious ways that beer can enliven any meal. These beers are just too good to leave in the kitchen when it comes time to eat!

A Final Word about Premium Beer

Like any other guidebook, the *Premium Beer Drinker's Guide* is designed to help mark a trail. In this case, the trail is the path of beer exploration, and it is an often winding and confusing one. The purpose of this book, then, is to help you navigate your personal path to beer-drinking bliss while avoiding the perils and pitfalls of mediocre beer scattered along the route.

To fully enjoy the journey, however, you need to be open to the endless possibilities that beer presents, such as the possibility that a classic beer might be brewed entirely from barley malt, hops, water and yeast, or that it might contain rye, coriander, barley kilned over peat, sugar, unmalted wheat, cherries or St. John's wort. It might be an ale of amber color, a jet-black stout, a pale golden wheat beer or a scarlet cherry beer. And it might very well be refreshingly spicy, determinedly dry, fortifyingly sweet or intriguingly complex.

The important thing to remember is that neither color nor style alone will determine whether a beer is poor, average or extraordinary. That determination rests on the skill and vision of the brewer, plus, of course, the quality of the ingredients and the efficiency of the brewery's equipment. Yet no matter how able a brewer may be, he or she still cannot guard against the preconceptions and prejudices of the beer drinker, so it is up to all of us to approach each and every beer with a clean palate and an open mind.

The global brewing industry knows few boundaries, and that simple fact is at once beer's greatest triumph and its most problematic trait. It means that so long as it is made from fermented grain, virtually any beverage may be called a beer, so the classic, Reinheitsgebot-pure lager from the historic Bavarian brewery is every bit as legitimate as the honey-almond-basil wheat ale from the two-person operation down the street. To decide whether you want one or the other, or neither or both, you must taste each one, and with thousands of breweries and tens of thousands of beers brewed around the world, that means a lot of sampling.

Some style guidelines do exist, and while styles such as amber ale and pilsner might be, and frequently are, subject to well-meaning but dramatic misinterpretation, premium beers such as abbey-style ales, eisbocks and barley wines are much less so. So where you might be getting anything from mildly malty ale to a hoppy monster in a bottle labeled "amber ale," at least you better know what you're getting into when the style listed is a premium one, such as those outlined on the following pages. (Exceptions to this generalization are discussed in certain style sections. Of particular note is the hefeweizen, whose meaning has been very broadly stretched by many North American craft breweries to the point that there is almost no telling whether a North American-brewed beer marked "weizen" will be spicy and fruity, or dull and earthy.)

So when you read this book, take note of the qualities presented by the different styles. Note which beers are good with food and which are more refreshing drunk alone; look for beers that are best in summer and those that would be better reserved for winter; and watch for their alcoholic strengths, all listed in percent by volume. You may wish to choose lower strengths for earlier in the day and the higher ones as a nightcap. Armed with all this knowledge, you will be able to purchase beers that will enhance your pleasure rather than just fill your glass.

Finally, and most importantly, keep trying new things. The hundreds of "Classic Examples" and other brands listed in this book are among the best of the styles they represent, but they by no means define their type. New brews continually appear on the market, and old ones disappear, and the only way to keep up with your beer appreciation is to take a chance occasionally. The new brew may be a dog or it may be a star, but you will never know for certain unless you try it.

Cheers!

MATCHING BEER AND FOOD

Here are four handy hints for general beer and food matching. They won't guarantee your results, but they will minimize the risk.

1. *Think of Ale as Red Wine and Lager as White Wine*

In other words, when red meat or any dish that you would normally pair with red wine is on the menu, select an ale to serve with it. Conversely, if the main course is fish or poultry, try a lager.

2. *Hoppiness in Beer = Acidity in Wine*

Anytime that you would seek a wine with high acidity — such as with spicy or oily food — choose a beer with significant hoppiness, or bitterness. The more acidic you would want the wine, the hoppier you will want the beer.

3. *Complement or Contrast*

Try to match foods to beers with complementary characters, such as a robust stew with a full-bodied ale. Or try a contrasting flavor, such as a crisp, refreshing lager with a heavy cream soup.

4. *Keep the Beer Sweeter than the Dessert*

Nothing kills the flavor of a beer like the overpowering sweetness of a dessert, so try to keep the sugar contents of both beer and dessert balanced. (Exceptions to this rule can be made for chocolate, which pairs well even with dry stout.)

Glossary

Ale

Ale is a top-fermented beer. Along with lager, it is one of the two main families of beer. Styles of ale include, but are not limited to, stout, best bitter, porter and barley wine. (See also top-fermentation.)

Bottle-Fermentation

Bottle-fermented beer, usually ale, is packaged with live yeast in order to produce a final fermentation in the bottle. Also known as bottle-conditioning, bottle-fermentation differs from unfiltered beer in that the yeast cells are active at the point of bottling.

Bottom-Fermentation

With top-fermentation, bottom-fermentation is one of the two types of fermentation that results in beer. Bottom-fermentation takes place at cooler temperatures and generally results in a cleaner, crisper-tasting beer that requires longer periods of maturing before it is ready for consumption. (See also lager.)

Brewkettle

A brewkettle is any vessel in which the wort is boiled and hops and/or other spices are added prior to fermentation.

Cask

In cask-conditioning, a cask is the keg in which beer is allowed to undergo a final fermentation prior to tapping and serving.

Cask-Conditioning

Cask-conditioning is the process in which beer, usually ale, undergoes a final fermentation in the cask from which it will eventually be served. Unlike conventional draft beer, cask-conditioned beer, commonly known as cask ale or real ale, is generally served without the use of additional gases.

Draft

Draft beer is served from the keg or cask, usually pressured through a draft tap by carbon dioxide or "beer gas," a mixture of nitrogen and carbon dioxide.

Dry-Hopping

Dry-hopping is the process whereby extra hops are added to beer, usually ale, following its primary fermentation. Dry-hopping generally produces a more aromatic beer.

Fermentation

Fermentation is the process by which yeast cells turn sugars into carbon dioxide and alcohol.

Fermenter

A fermenter is any vessel in which the wort is placed for fermentation.

Hops

Hops are the cones of the plant *Humulus lupulus.* They were originally added to beer for their preservative effect, but are now used mainly for bitterness and aroma. Dozens if not hundreds of varieties of hops are in use in brewing today.

Keg

A keg is the container from which draft beer is served. Kegs come in many sizes, but the most common ones hold 50 or 58.6 liters (13.2 or 15.5 gallons) of beer.

Lager

Lager is bottom-fermented beer. Along with ale, it is one of the two main families of beer. Styles of lager include, but are not limited to, pilsner, bock, doppelbock and märzen. (See also bottom-fermentation.)

Malt

Malt is barley or other grains that are soaked in water until they begin to sprout, thereby releasing starches that will later be converted into sugars during the mash. Following this germination, the grains are kilned to halt the growth. The malt may then be further kilned to anything from a sandy gold to chocolate brown color, or even roasted black, to produce different flavors and colors.

MASH

During the mash, the malt is steeped in hot water, converting the grain's starches into fermentable sugars.

MASH TUN

The mash tun is the large, open-topped vessel in which the mash takes place.

PASTEURIZATION

Pasteurization is a process whereby beer is super-heated in order to kill any microorganisms that may be present.

TOP-FERMENTATION

With bottom-fermentation, top-fermentation is one of the two types of fermentation that results in beer. Top-fermentation takes place at warmer temperatures and generally results in a fruitier beer that is ready for consumption after a shorter period of maturation. (See also ale.)

UNFILTERED

Unfiltered beer, usually ale, is bottled without first undergoing a strict filtration. Typically this results in a beer that will appear slightly to some-what hazy in the glass. Unfiltered beer differs from bottle-conditioned beer in that the yeast cells that will be present in the beer are inactive and so will not produce a new fermentation.

WORT

Wort is the "sugar water," or unfermented beer, that results from the mash.

All of the beers mentioned in the following style sections are highly recommended examples of their type, particularly those listed in the "Classic Examples" sections. Each "Classic Example" listing comes with an information key to help you shop. It tells you not only what beers to buy, but roughly how much each one will cost, how long it will last in peak form and how easy or difficult it may be to find.

PRICE RANGE

Compared to a six-pack of run-of-the-mill brew, all of the beers cited in this guide are expensive. On the other hand, compared to a bottle of mediocre wine, almost all are cheap. The important point is to view the cost in relation to the quality of the beer, a practice that makes every one of these premium beers not just good, but a great value.

Because so many variables affect price – currency fluctuations, pricing policies that vary from store to store, state to state and province to province, differences in bottle size and variable taxation rates – it is difficult to suggest specific prices for each of the recommended beers. For this reason, the Price Range is intended to give only a very general idea of how much each beer is likely to cost.

Price Range is indicated by these symbols:

$	moderately more than the price of an ordinary domestic beer
$ $	roughly two to three times the price of an ordinary domestic beer
$ $ $	more than three times the price of an ordinary domestic beer

FRESHNESS & DURABILITY

Almost all beer is best consumed within about three to six months of packaging, providing that it has been stored under favorable conditions. Some beers, however, stand the test of time better than others, and some will even benefit from months or years of aging. The Freshness & Durability guide, then, will give you a rough idea of how much time you have to enjoy your premium beer.

When storing beer, circumstance is a vital consideration. For short-term holding, keep your beer in the refrigerator. For long-term cellaring, keep the beer in a cool, dark, odor-free place and keep the temperature as consistent as possible. It is better to keep beer in a cellar that stays at a consistent 12°C (54°F) than in one that fluctuates seasonally between 7°C (45°F) and 16°C (61°F). Store capped beer upright and corked beer on its side, as you would a bottle of wine.

Freshness & Durability are indicated by these symbols:

✳	a youthful treat; drink as fresh as possible
✳ ✳	durable and delicious; will easily last up to a year in the cellar
✳ ✳ ✳	fabulous young or old; will age nicely for at least several years in the cellar
✳ ✳ ✳ ✳	a rare classic; at its best after five or more years of aging

AVAILABILITY

The constantly changing face of the beer market makes it extremely difficult to predict the availability of various beers, and the interests of breweries, the actions of importers and the vagaries of regional legislation make it that much harder. Nonetheless, some beers are undeniably easier to find than others, and the "Availability" guide gives you a general idea of how hard you have to look to find each beer.

For the majority of the "Classic Examples," the beer is available only in the bottle, usually packaged in a 355 mL (12-oz), 500 mL (17-oz) or 750 mL (25-oz) size. Most domestically brewed beer is also available on draft, as are some of the imported brands, but the highly regionalized distribution of kegged beer makes it impossible to say which brews will be on tap in your area. My advice is to locate one or two good local beer bars and keep up-to-date on what they have on draft.

The Availability ranking is based purely on the ease or difficulty I have had finding these beers in various cities and towns across Canada and the United States. If you have trouble finding a specific beer, call or write the brewery directly (brewery information is listed at the back of the book) or search the Internet. (One good place to start a search is the Real Beer Page at http://www.realbeer.com.) Without exception, however, all of the "Classic Examples" are well worth the hunt!

Availability is indicated by these symbols:

✓	be prepared to search long and hard
✓ ✓	likely only to be found in specialty shops
✓ ✓ ✓	might require a couple of stops before you find it
✓ ✓ ✓ ✓	hardly ubiquitous, but fairly widely available

THE
SHIP INN
AT
SHAFTESBURY

Badger Beer

BAR FOOD

WE ARE IN...
THE GOOD PUB. GUIDE 97
THE QUIET PINT GUIDE 97

TRY US FOR WONDERFUL FOOD, GREAT
BEERS, GOOD CONVERSATION & A REAL
WELCOME.
BAR MENU & DAILY SPECIALS.

Wessex alarms

MORNING COFFEE
FULL BAR
RESTAURANT

WHERE THE WILD YEASTS ARE

Within the past decade or two, many attempts
have been made by breweries large and small
to replicate the beers of the past. From Anchor
Brewing's Sumerian recipe Ninkasi beer to Scottish and Newcastle's purported replication of an
ale from Tutankhamen's time, there is something
about the archeology and anthropology of their
craft that continues to fascinate modern brewers.

Then there are the ancient styles that have
never changed: the spontaneously fermented and
wood-conditioned beers of Belgium. These beers
speak of a time when fermentation was only tan-
gentially understood and the idea of controlling
the microbiology of brewing was so distant that
it could not even be dreamt of. These brews need
not replicate history; they are history.

To the modern brewer, absolute control over fermentation is as fundamental and essential to brewing as breathing is to life. Breweries today have labs and, in some cases, entire company divisions dedicated to monitoring the yeasts they use and assuring that no contamination or mutation is allowed to occur. Some breweries are so fastidious that they do not even allow a second brewing yeast culture to enter the building, lest it mix with their primary yeast and result in off-flavors and potentially the ruination of entire fermenters full of beer.

Even amid this modern, highly controlled global brewing culture, however, there still exist brewers who not only tolerate the arrival of wild yeast, they encourage it. They are the lambic brewers of Belgium, a handful of dedicated artisans gathered in a cluster of breweries located in the Zenne Valley around Brussels. And the beers that they brew are some of the most complex and intriguing in the world.

Before Louis Pasteur's seminal work with brewing yeasts, fermentation was only vaguely understood. The first creators of beer, who lived more than 5,000 years ago, understood only that water and grain mixed together and left alone would eventually become fizzy and flavorful, and would make their imbiber feel quite good. Much later, brewers discovered that beers left in cold caves would develop different properties than those left in warmer places, and so lager fermentation was born. Then Pasteur made it possible to isolate yeast cultures and more closely control fermentation. That was the beginning of the end for wild yeasts in brewing.

However, lambic brewing with wild yeast persisted, and for many years the resulting beverage remained the people's beer in Flemish Belgium. In its creation, raw wheat is mixed with malted barley in the mash, aged hops are used for their preservative qualities rather than their flavor, and fermentation is accomplished by opening up the windows and rooftop louvers to allow wild,

airborne yeasts to have their way with the wort. Once fermentation has
been completed, the beer is then transferred to wooden casks, themselves
repositories of various microflora, and aged for one to three years. The
resulting beer is known as lambic.

Because of its unusual method of fermentation, each batch of lambic
is different. This inconsistency is corrected by the blender, who carefully
matches up casks of different ages to produce a beer of more or less
consistent flavor. This blended brew is known as gueuze, and it is bottled
unfiltered with a small amount of unfermented wort added to promote a
final bottle-fermentation.

Lambic brewers today vary in their adherence to tradition. Jean-Pierre
Van Roy at Brasserie Cantillon in Brussels, for example, is a committed purist
who will neither control his fermentation nor sweeten his gueuze. As a result,
his lambics are considered by many to be the most authentic and treasured,
and although that may be debatable, the fact that they are the most tart, acidic
and assertive is not. Other traditionalists include Jean Hanssens; Frank Boon,
a brewer and blender from Lembeek; Armand de Belder, a chef-turned-
blender who runs the Drie Fonteinen restaurant in the Brussels suburb of
Beersel; and the revivalist lambic blender and brewer Willem Van Herreweghe
of De Cam.

Other lambic brewers and blenders (some producers buy their lambics
from various breweries and blend the product themselves) are more open to
a modern interpretation of the art of the gueuze. For example, the filtering
and sweetening of the beer, as seen in the popular Belle-Vue, Mort Subite and
Lindemans gueuzes and fruit lambics, takes away the tart edge and makes the
beer more accessible to the general public. It also, unfortunately, has a delete-
rious effect on the marvelous character of a "raw" gueuze, which is never
sweet and should always have a yeast sediment in the bottle.

CANTILLON GUEUZE

Price: $$$
Freshness & Durability: ✳ ✳ ✳
Availability: ✓ ✓

For any beer aficionado with an interest in lambic, a visit to the Cantillon brewery in Brussels is a must. There, in an industrial sector of the city a short distance from the Gare du Midi train station, Jean-Pierre Van Roy crafts some of the world's most distinctive and challenging beers, using brewing equipment up to 100 years old. A tour of Cantillon is one of the most fascinating brewery tours offered anywhere, providing an intimate look at the way brewing once was and, at Cantillon at least, still is.

The brewery tour ends, as most do, with a tasting of the beer. Having been so romanced by the building, it is hard to believe that anyone could resist the charms of the beverage brewed within its walls, yet the Cantillon beer is still not to some tastes. But this is no ordinary brew.

Cantillon's gueuze is without question the world's most aggressive. Newcomers to the realm of spontaneously fermented beers are advised to approach it with caution, for as much as Cantillon's overwhelmingly tart, acidic character is treasured by those familiar with it, it can also come as a shock to anyone led to a glass unprepared. The true joy of the beer comes below the tartness, though, in a complex, almost creamy mix of earthy, fruity and barnyardy notes. Excellent with steamed mussels, it also provides a marvelous contrasting taste to strong, salty cheeses. On its own, it is a fine summer refresher.

HANSSENS OUDE GUEUZE

Price: $$$
Freshness & Durability: ✳ ✳ ✳
Availability: ✓ ✓

Brewed and bottled by:
Hanssens Artisanaal
since 1896
Dworp, Belgium

Oude Gueuze
Lambic

Each bottle matured for over three years

Imported by B. United International, Elmsford, NY 10523

750 ML OF BEER · 1 PINT 10.4 FL OZ.
PRODUCT OF BELGIUM

CA REDEMPTION VALUE CT-ME-VT-DE-MA-NY-IA-OR-5C* MI 10¢ REFUND

GOVERNMENT WARNING: (1) ACCORDING TO THE SURGEON GENERAL, WOMEN SHOULD NOT DRINK ALCOHOLIC BEVERAGES DURING PREGNANCY BECAUSE OF THE RISK OF BIRTH DEFECTS. (2) CONSUMPTION OF ALCOHOLIC BEVERAGES IMPAIRS YOUR ABILITY TO DRIVE A CAR OR OPERATE MACHINERY, AND MAY CAUSE HEALTH PROBLEMS.

If any gueuze even begins to approach the assertiveness of the Cantillon, it is that of Jean Hanssens, a gueuze blender from the Belgian town of Dworp. Hanssens' beers have been for years the holy grail of gueuze aficionados worldwide, since production is so limited that they are difficult to find even in Belgium. In style, they are reassuringly tart, dry (but not to the point of austerity) and very well structured, with just enough fruity, lemony notes (from fermentation, not fruit additions) to lend them a balanced complexity.

Being a blender and not a brewer, Hanssens relies on the lambics produced by others, which in his case are Lindemans, Boon and Girardin. Yet it is his skill in managing the casks and blending together their contents that places his signature upon the finished product and creates his masterpiece.

Along with coveting bottles of Hanssens Gueuze, beer lovers also feared for the future of the brand. They did so because as Jean Hanssens prepared to retire, there appeared to be no heir to take over his gueuze blending tradition. Fortunately, in 1998, word arrived that Jean's daughter, Cindy Matthys, and her husband, John, were ready and determined to continue Jean's work and maintain the patriarch's high standards. And so the future of this classic gueuze appears secure.

FRUIT LAMBIC

It is a safe bet that fruit of one variety or another has been used to flavor beer since brewing's earliest days. Lacking control over which wild yeasts would ferment their beers, ancient Egyptian and Sumerian brewers probably used spices or fruit, or perhaps both, to cover up the off-flavors that inevitably arose. This practice no doubt continued sporadically throughout the history of brewing.

The practice continues today in the form of fruit lambics, although the fruits employed today are not added to cover up flavor so much as to add depth and character to the beers.

It is difficult to say when the modern tradition of kriek (cherry lambic) and framboise (raspberry lambic) began, but the common wisdom suggests that the former preceded the latter by a great many years. This might well not be the case. Jean-Pierre Van Roy, brewer and owner of the great Brussels lambic brewery, Cantillon, has produced documents from 1909 showing that his brewery had stock of both kriek and framboise at that time, proving that framboise is not the recent invention it is sometimes thought to be. Regardless of which came first, however, there is no doubt that these two are the original fruit lambics.

The way a traditional kriek or framboise is produced is as interesting as the beer itself. Once the lambic has been brewed, fermented and transferred into wooden casks, the conditioning is allowed to continue for as much as a year or more, until the brewer or blender feels that the beer's character has sufficiently evolved. Whole fruit is then added directly to the cask, and buoyed by the new sources of sugars (from the fruit) and yeast (from the skins), fermentation begins all over again. After an additional three to six months of conditioning, the beer is blended with some young lambic to provoke bottle-fermentation, corked and capped and left to mature further in the bottle.

Unfortunately, in recent years tradition has been increasingly ignored in fruit lambic production. A growing number of lambic breweries now use fruit syrups rather than whole fruit to flavor the beer, and the conditioning time has been dropped drastically. Certain modern-day krieks and framboises, such as the Belle-Vue Kriek and St. Louis Framboise, bear no more than a passing similarity to the authentic, traditional product.

Another recent trend, one that has led to very mixed results, has been the use of nontraditional fruits and other flavorings in lambic beers. At the more questionable end of the scale lies the de Troch line of lambics bottled under the Chapeau name, including pineapple- and banana-flavored beers, and the Lindemans Tea Beer, which includes in its ingredients tea leaves, tea flavor and lemon juice. On the slightly more conventional and, to my taste, enjoyable side of things, the Mort Subite line of sweetened lambics, for example, reaches its zenith with an appetizing Cassis, a lightly tart, dry-ish aperitif beer flavored with black currant.

More traditional lambic brewers also create some wonderful fruit beers, but they unfortunately tend to be very hard to find. Perhaps the finest kriek I have tasted came from the Oud Beersel brewery in the town of the same name near Brussels, and that is likely the only place it can be found. The small lambic brewery Girardin likewise makes a nice kriek, as do De Cam and Drie Fonteinen, but again these are only sporadically available in certain bars and cafés, all in Belgium.

Some North American breweries have leaped into the lambic field over the past few years, albeit using laboratory-cultured *Brettanomyaces*, or lambic yeast strains, rather than trusting whatever might be flying around wild in their neighborhoods. I have tasted a barnyardy orange lambic at Storm Brewing in Vancouver, British Columbia, as well as a fine blackberry lambic at the Diamondback Brewery brewpub in Cleveland, Ohio, where they have the wonderful luxury of a stone crawl space in their cellar in which to age their wooden casks properly.

BOON MARIAGE PARFAIT KRIEK

Price: $$$
Freshness & Durability: ✳ ✳ ✳
Availability: ✓

Mariage Parfait is French for "perfect marriage," and that is what Frank Boon thinks he has when he bottles these particularly well-balanced, harmonious lambics. This is not to say that Boon's ordinary gueuze, kriek and framboise, bottled under the plain F. Boon label, are anything to sneer at: they are fine, if somewhat mild-mannered, examples of the lambic blender's art. But when Boon hits a blend that works particularly well, he's not afraid to brag about it, to all lambic lovers' advantage.

Having begun his lambic life as a blender, Boon turned to brewing his own in 1990 and has experienced a fair amount of success in so doing. Based in Lembeek, the town that legend declares gave lambic its name, Boon is well known and respected for the Mariage Parfait line, which includes Geuze (Boon uses an alternative spelling) as well as Framboise and Kriek.

While an F. Boon Kriek tends toward an off-dry, highly fruity character, a Mariage Parfait demonstrates much more of the traditional lambic character. While not as abstemious in fruit flavor as certain other fruit lambics, some of which show only nuances of the fruit, the Mariage Parfait Kriek is a dry, slightly tart beer with a healthy amount of fruit in both the flavor and aroma. Indeed, it is the perfect marriage between fruit flavor and lambic tradition.

CANTILLON
ROSÉ DE GAMBRINUS

Price: $$$
Freshness & Durability: ✳ ✳ ✳
Availability: ✓ ✓

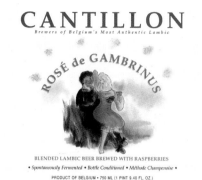

People who have sampled the Rosé only outside Belgium run the risk of forming a misguided opinion of it. The fruit aroma and flavor of this classic beer is so soft and nuanced and the lambic character so utterly and unapologetically aggressive that time is not exactly its best friend. And since plentiful amounts of time often pass between the sale of the beer in Brussels and its consumption overseas, Rosés tasted in North America sometimes have little fruit character left in them.

Tasted fresh, the Rosé is the proverbial iron fist in the velvet glove. The "iron" in this case is the wonderfully tart, assertive lambic of Cantillon, a classic base to which a mix of roughly three-quarters raspberries and one-quarter cherries – the "velvet" – is added. The result is a beer of exquisite character, with a perfumey, lightly vanilla-ish raspberry aroma mixing with the lambic's naturally fruity notes, and a sweet-and-sour berry flavor blending with the citric tang of the spontaneously fermented ale. Not a lambic for those who love only the taste of fruit in their beer, but a classic for those who appreciate balance in life.

Saint Lamvinus
1995

CANTILLON ST. LAMVINUS

Price: $$$
Freshness & Durability: ✳ ✳ ✳
Availability: ✓

In selecting the classic beers to feature in this book, two elements figured foremost. First and above all, I decided that the beer should be a true classic of its style, a great beer that speaks in flavor, aroma and character to everything that makes the style great. Secondly, I wanted to feature beers that are at least incidentally available outside their home towns, provinces and, preferably, countries.

So why, then, have I chosen as a classic fruit lambic a beer that is virtually unattainable outside Brussels? Simply because it is perhaps the finest lambic and one of the greatest beers I have ever tasted.

The experiment that led to the St. Lamvinus began in the early 1990s when Jean-Pierre Van Roy of Cantillon made arrangements to referment his lambic with grapes from the famed St. Emillon region of Bordeaux. The grape mix was the classic Bordeaux blend of cabernet sauvignon, cabernet franc and cabernet merlot; the beer was classic Cantillon.

I first tasted the resulting beer at seven years of age in 1997, and it was fabulous. The aroma was unquestionably lambic, but the flavor was magnificently complex, with typical lambic tartness and fruit in front but a startlingly dry, robust cabernet character in the finish. It was a beer I could have spent hours tasting, and still never have been fully satisfied with my notes.

Van Roy was fermenting and conditioning the second St. Lamvinus as I tasted the first, and it was released about one year later. When I encountered it in the fall of 1998, it hadn't quite developed the character of its older brother, but it was still a great beer. In either guise, the St. Lamvinus is well deserving of the title "classic."

Exposure to airborne microorganisms is normally the brewer's worst nightmare. Over the centuries, more than a few batches of beer have had to be dumped because of infection caused by wild bacteria, and no doubt many more will be dumped in the future. For certain styles of beer, however, the souring that goes along with such contaminations is not to be avoided but relished. Among these are the red and brown ales of Flanders.

To reach the roots of the Flemish brown and red ale tradition, one must travel back to at least the 18th century when beer was commonly stored in wood casks. At that time, English porters were regularly aged for months in wood, and the resultant exposure to air through the cask and to microflora within the wood of the cask would slightly sour the beer. The effect was to make the porter more refreshing and less obviously malty.

In northern Belgium, the same process was in place, except instead of aging all the beer and selling it as such, the Flemish brewers blended the aged beer with a younger brew and promoted a new fermentation. In western Flanders, these beers developed into the style known today as the Flemish red ale; in the east, the beer became oud bruin, or old brown ale.

While it is likely that both beers were originally fermented and aged in wood, that is no longer the case. The accepted route for the Flemish red is a primary fermentation in modern fermenters and a secondary conditioning in well-worn wooden tanks — not modestly sized casks, but massive oak vessels. At the brewery known for their classic red ale, Rodenbach, the young beer gets no wood aging at all while the older beer spends up to two years in the wooden tanks.

Fewer and fewer old browns even touch wood these days, although some smaller breweries around the town of Oudenaard are said to persist in the practice. Instead, today's Flemish old brown ales derive their tartness from a lactic culture that is incorporated into the fermentation inoculation, a process that provides the effect of the wood but with greater control. For this reason, some beer scholars argue that the old brown and Flemish red are stylistically different, while others say that their common roots prove that they are one and the same. I am inclined to side with the proponents of the latter school, but prefer enjoying the flavors of these ales to arguing about them.

With their tremendous complexity, tart characters and enticing flavors, both Flemish reds and old browns make terrific food beers. Both pair excellently with braised or stewed beef – beer writer Michael Jackson suggests that the old brown is the ideal beer for the classic Belgian dish carbonnade flamande – and to my mind, partner even better with horse or game, particularly when cooked or served with fruit. Rare among food-oriented beers, many red and brown ales serve as excellent aperitifs as well.

For the same reason that brewers outside Belgium are disinclined to brew lambics, few non-Belgian breweries make attempts at replicating the Flemish red or old brown style. Simply, most commercial brewers are afraid that the intentional souring of the Belgian-style brews could potentially cause an accidental infection of their other brands. For a brewery not specializing in Flemish red and old brown ales, that could be a business-ending nightmare.

The dangers do not seem to dissuade Belgian brewers, though, and many breweries in that country produce beers in either or both of the red and brown styles as well as several other styles. The well-soured Duchesse de Bourgogne from Verhaeghe of Vichte, for example, is a red brewed in the same place as a pilsner; the Strubbe brewery still produces their Ichtegems Oud Bruin at the same plant as they do their Strubbe Stout; and prior to a recent sweetening of the beer under the brand's current Riva ownership, the Gouden Carolus of the Anker-Carolus brewery of Mechelen was a classic old brown in its own right, brewed under the same roof as other, non-soured brown ales.

RODENBACH GRAND CRU

Price: $$$
Freshness & Durability: ✳ ✳ ✳
Availability: ✓ ✓

If the Flemish red and old brown styles are indeed descendants of the same beer, the Rodenbach brewery unquestionably sits atop the family tree. In fact, the Liefmans yeast is even said to be an offspring of the original Rodenbach strain, a fact that would seem to give credence to those who say the styles are in fact one and the same.

The "regular" Rodenbach, the one marketed without the Grand Cru nomenclature, is a blend of old and young Flemish red ale. The old is aged for up to two years in oak and constitutes about one-quarter of the mix; the young touches no wood and makes up the rest. Both are fermented by the house yeast, which today is no fewer than 22 separate, identifiable strains.

The Grand Cru is the pure, old ale. The wood in which it has sat for so long is immediately in evidence when a glass filled with the "Burgundy of Belgium" is raised to the lips. A potent bouquet of sour cherry and old oak fills the nostrils and immediately sets the mouth to watering. Then the taste; puckering at first, followed by a rich, fruity tartness that both cleanses the palate and quenches the thirst. Arguably too bold to be served as an aperitif (although it would perhaps appeal to Campari drinkers), the Grand Cru is nonetheless fine drinking on a summer's eve and excellent beside a seasonal salad.

LIEFMANS GOUDENBAND

Price: $$$
Freshness & Durability: ✳ ✳ ✳
Availability: ✓ ✓

As Rodenbach is to the Flemish red style, so Liefmans is to the old brown. It is the authentic and definitive article, each bottle filled as much with history and legend as with barley and hops. And as the Grand Cru is to the Rodenbach brewery, so the Goudenband is to Liefmans, with the exception that it does not spend as long maturing and is not bottled "straight," but rather blended with a younger ale.

The Goudenband has perhaps lost some of its trademark sour "bite" over the years, but the sharpness brought on by the lactic culture is still very much in evidence. The aroma offers plentiful notes of sour cherry, even to the point that many tasters mistake the Goudenband for a fruit beer. (Liefmans also makes a fine Frambozenbier flavored with raspberries and a very satisfying cherry-flavored Kriek, each of which have added fruit and which may contribute to this popular misconception.) The body provides a sweet-and-sour flavor with a dignified, slightly nutty malt background.

While some beer aficionados have proposed that the Goudenband no longer ages well, the five- to seven-year-old versions I have tasted of late belie that notion. One five-year-old bottle in particular was impressive, with round, dried fruit notes and a character well suited to an after-dinner selection of hard and soft cheeses.

WHY NOT WHEAT?

The majority of beer produced around the globe today is made from malted barley. Many large, international breweries, and more than a few small ones, use portions of rice, corn or other fermentable grains and sugars to make their beer. Between them these portions may constitute up to one-third of the total weight of the grist, but at its heart most beer has barley.

It has not always been this way. In re-creating the beer of Tutankhamen from evidence discovered in a well-preserved ancient Egyptian village, the brewing company Scottish and Newcastle found that they needed to brew from a strain of wheat known as Emmer. And from that 3,500-year-old brew, it is but a surprisingly short jump to the wheat beers of today: German-style Hefeweizen, Belgian-style White Beer, and in a blend of Bavarian beer styles, strong Weizenbock.

Hefeweizen

To anyone raised in the "wait until the sun is over the yardarm" school of never having a beer before noon, a breakfast beer is likely to be associated only with a serious drinking problem. They forget that for most of its many millennia of existence beer has been viewed as liquid bread, appropriate as a substitute for, or complement to, a meal taken at any time of the day. If that meant a pint or a quart (or two) supped before heading out into the fields in the morning, then so be it.

The Germans, particularly those of the southern region of Bavaria, one of the great beer-drinking districts of the world, have not forgotten this. In fact, they laud and in many places uphold en masse the custom of the midmorning brew. And as often as not, they do so with a hefeweizen.

The German word *weizen* means wheat, while the prefix *hefe-* denotes yeast. Put these together and you get a hefeweizen, a wheat beer with yeast in it. But it is more than that. Also known as weissbier – *weiss* meaning white – hefeweizen has been enjoyed in southern Germany for hundreds of years. Its earliest recorded period of intense popularity occurred during the first half of the 17th century, when the Bavarian Duke Maximilian I held the exclusive license to brew hefeweizen and so promoted its consumption in order to fill his treasury and finance his war against the rival Wallenstein family.

By the middle of the 19th century, however, hefeweizen had lost so much favor among the populace that the rulers of Bavaria no longer found it financially beneficial to maintain their iron grip on its production. And so, in 1856, a brewer named Georg Schneider was able to take over the lease on the royal court's Weisses Brauhaus, or white beer brewery. Later, in 1872, Schneider recognized that the other, adjacent royal brewery required more space and offered to vacate the brewery in exchange for the termination of the royal wheat beer prerogative. His terms were met and so ended 250 years of royal wheat beer exclusivity, and began the Schneider wheat beer brewery.

The beer style that Schneider returned to the citizenry is a light to medium gold brew that is often quite cloudy in appearance. (This characteristic haze, which results from the addition of yeast to the beer at the bottling stage, is not only normal but also healthful, containing as it does a wealth of complex B vitamins.) Because of the specific family of top-fermenting yeasts used, a true hefeweizen will also have clovey, peppery and fruity (banana-like or bubblegummy) notes to the aroma, as well as similar flavors in the body. It will also be very effervescent, refreshing and highly enjoyable.

Most major southern German brewers still produce a hefeweizen. In Munich, Spaten makes the Franziskaner Hefe-Weissbier, dry and spicy with a hint of banana, while just outside the city, the Andechs monastery is respected for their very clovey, spicy Andechser Weissbier. A little farther from Munich in Aying can be found the Ayinger brewery and their fruity Ur-Weiss, and farther still, in Nuremberg, Tucher offers an appley Helles Hefeweizen. In the city of Bamberg, famous for its rauchbier, Zum Spezial brews a peppery, clovey, smoked malt Weizen.

Hefeweizens abound elsewhere as well. In Japan, the Kiuchi Brewery of Ibaraki produces a highly spicy hefeweizen under the Hitachino Nest label. In the United States, the Tabernash Brewing Company of Denver, Colorado, has made a name for itself with the citrusy Tabernash Weiss, while Maryland's Baltimore Brewing brings Bavaria to Charm City with their bubblegummy DeGroen's Weizen. Residents of Toronto, Ontario, delight in the balanced fruit-spice Weizen of the Denison's Brewing Company brewpub.

SCHNEIDER WEISSE

Price: $$
Freshness & Durability: ✱ ✱
Availability: ✓ ✓ ✓

For those who place some stock in tradition, it is always satisfying when the progenitor of a certain type or style of product remains the best, even over a century or more. And so it is in the case of Schneider Weiss, which to my mind is still the finest hefeweizen.

The two breweries in which the original Georg Schneider brewed still stand in Munich – the first has been turned into the famed Hofbrauhaus, and the second, the Weisses Brauhaus, now operates as a sort of displaced "brewery tap" for Schneider – but the beer is produced at a facility in nearby Kelheim. Nonetheless, the Weisses Brauhaus at Tal Strasse 10 does provide perhaps the ultimate hefeweizen experience, as you sit amid the never-ending hustle and bustle typical of Munich's huge beerhalls, sipping on a half-liter of delightfully spicy (clove, cinnamon, nutmeg) and fruity (hints of citrus and banana) draft Schneider Weisse.

Not everybody can make it to Munich each time they desire a hefeweizen, so it is fortunate that one of the great things about hefeweizen is that it travels well. The complex, balanced and rewarding flavors concocted by the fifth generation of Schneiders are just as fine in the bottle at home as they are at the beerhall in Munich – only a bit less atmospheric.

WEIHENSTEPHANER HEFEWEISSBIER

Price: $$
Freshness & Durability: ✳ ✳
Availability: ✓ ✓ ✓

The Bayerische Staatsbrauerei Weihenstephan in Freising, Germany, is reputed to be the oldest brewery in the world, dating from 1040. And although it is unclear how many operational stoppages may have occurred during that time or how long they may have lasted, it is certainly true that few breweries today can lay claim to a legacy anywhere near that long. For the contemplative beer drinker, then, cracking open a bottle of Weihenstephaner beer is a bit like a journey back through time.

There is much more than just history and nostalgia in each bottle of Weihenstephaner Hefeweissbier. When fresh, it is famously fruity, with a citrus-banana nose and a complex orange-apple-banana body that has even been said to carry light currant notes. The finish brings the underlying spice of the flavor to the fore, drying the taste and making the beer perfect for Sunday brunches or Saturday afternoons on the patio. It is particularly wonderful with the German veal sausage, weisswurst.

Weihenstephan is also home to the world's most famous brewing school and, as such, exports much more than just its beer. Graduates of the Technical University of Munich in Weinhenstephan operate the breweries of companies all over the world, and techniques learned there influence the way much of the beer produced by those breweries is made. Even the yeast is well traveled; the Weihenstephan strain is perhaps the single most popular weizen yeast among North American brewers of German-style wheats, be they grads of the famous school or not.

The Belgians are the original innovators of the beer world. You may recall my mention of the German Reinheitsgebot, the Bavarian law that limits beer's ingredients to water, hops, malt and yeast. Well, the Belgians take a somewhat contrary position, incorporating almost everything but the proverbial kitchen sink in their brews.

The white beer, also known as wit or bière blanche, is no exception to this rule, being spiced with coriander and orange peel, plus occasional "secret ingredients" known only to the brewer. It is also made with a very healthy proportion of unmalted wheat – as much as half of the total grain used – which gives the beer a light and consummately refreshing flavor.

In its use of coriander, white beer harkens back to the earliest recorded days of brewing. The most popular seasoning in the world, coriander was among the ingredients in the Tutankhamen Ale crafted by Scottish and Newcastle, following a recipe pieced together by archeobotanists from the well-preserved ruins of an ancient Egyptian brewery.

Yet despite this noble lineage, white beer was almost lost to the world when it fell out of fashion in the mid-20th century. Thanks to one young brewer in northern Belgium who believed in the future of white beer, though, the style has enjoyed a worldwide renaissance. That young man's name was Pierre Celis. And the brewery he founded in 1966 and in which he revived the pale golden white beer was called De Kluis, "The Cloister," but it became much better known for the name of its most popular brand, Hoegaarden White. Not long after Celis started producing his white beer, other breweries in Belgium realized that they had better follow suit or miss out on the growing market for the style. Thus, a white beer boom was born.

A fire at the brewery in 1985 almost brought the Hoegaarden White's life to a very premature end, but fortunately Celis was able to secure an equity investment from the Belgian brewing concern Interbrew and rebuild his brewery. This arrangement continued for a few years until Celis decided to bring white beer brewing to another country. In 1991 he moved to Texas to open the Celis Brewery in Austin.

The popularity of white beer in North America, Belgium and across Europe has hardly faltered since. One reason is likely the beer's refreshing character, a result of the way the citric flavors of the unmalted wheat blend with the spice of the coriander and the fruitiness of the orange peel and top-fermenting yeast. It's a combination that makes white beer wonderful as an aperitif, particularly during the summer, and the ideal beer for brunch.

As might be expected, numerous Belgian breweries produce very fine interpretations of the style, including Gouden Boom's soft, orangey Blanche de Bruges from the Flemish city of that name, Van Eecke's lemony Watou's Witbier, also named for the brewery's home town, and the fuller-bodied, comparatively rich Blanche des Honnelles from the pious-sounding but quite secular brewery Abbaye des Rocs in Montignies-sur-Roc.

White beers remain popular elsewhere in Europe as well. The Netherlands and northern France, in particular, produce several fine interpretations, including the fragrant Amadeus of Les Brasseurs de Gayant of Douai, France. Nowhere outside Belgium, however, has the style caught on quite as it has in North America.

The first white beer brewed in the New World was the dry, mildly spicy Blanche de Chambly from the Chambly, Quebec, brewer Unibroue. It was followed by several other Quebec whites, including the peppery, slightly honeyed Bière Blanche Originale of the Brasserie Cheval Blanc of Montreal. In the United States the Celis White leads the way, but Belgian wheat beers such as the well-coriandered, if confusingly named, Hefeweizen from Rogue Ales of Newport, Oregon, and the slightly tart Sunshine Wheat Beer of Fort Collins, Colorado's New Belgium Brewing are also contenders.

HOEGAARDEN

Price: $$
Freshness & Durability: ✳
Availability: ✓ ✓ ✓

Because its brewery is owned by Interbrew, one of the largest brewing companies in the world, many beer aficionados are tempted to write off the modern-day Hoegaarden, theorizing that no big brewer could possibly turn out a white beer of character and distinction. In many, if not most, instances, I would be tempted to agree, but in the case of the Hoegaarden White, such generalizations are invalid. In fact, to indulge in such big-brewery stereotyping in this case would be to deny oneself one of the delights of the world of beer.

The beauty of the Hoegaarden White lies in the delicate balance it strikes between the spice and the fruit. The nose offers plenty of coriander on top of a mildly fruity base, while the body reverses that with citrusy orange notes fronting a softly spicy background. The result is a beer that is both refreshing and satisfying, mild enough for afternoon thirst-quenching yet sufficiently complex to tempt the most critical palate.

I do not believe that this Hoegaarden White is the same as the one I was introduced to in 1987, but neither do I think it deserving of the blanket condemnations it sometimes receives from highly critical and perhaps slightly paranoid beer aficionados. By any measure, this is still one of the world's great beers.

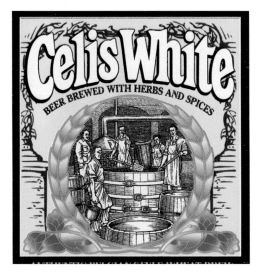

CELIS WHITE

Price: $
Freshness & Durability: ∗
Availability: ✓ ✓ ✓

As the father of the revival of white beer, Pierre Celis carries heavy clout in the beer world. Those searching for proof of this need look no further than the fact that Pierre originally sold his brewery to the massive brewing company Interbrew, then moved his talents to Austin, Texas, and subsequently sold his new brewery in 1995, this time to Miller, all without a peep of skepticism from the normally distrustful legions of brewing traditionalists.

And so it is that the two classic whites were originally formulated by the same man. It is somewhat surprising, therefore, that Celis White and Hoegaarden White are in some ways the yin and yang of white beers. Where Hoegaarden leads with its coriandered aroma, Celis offers a big orange blossom nose with much more mild hints of spice in the background. The citric character continues in the taste of the Celis White, but not so much as to make the beer lose its refreshing nature.

After Celis sold a majority stake in his Texas brewery to Miller Brewing of Milwaukee, Wisconsin, some observers noted significant changes in the beers. For his part, Celis denies his accusers, saying that his daughter and son-in-law, who still run the brewery, are making the same beer he brewed when he first started in Texas. And to my taste, he's more or less right, save perhaps for a slight increase in the perfumey orange character of the beer.

The world of beer is a challenging one, at times as confounding as it is delightful. Unlike the wine industry, which is relatively well governed by rules dictating what wine makers may and may not do, the beer business sometimes seems almost anarchic in nature. Just when you think that you have a handle on, say, the ins and outs of fermentation and how they define whether a beer is an ale or a lager, along comes a brewery with a top-fermented "lager," bottom-fermented "ale," or some other confusing combination.

This confusion even reigns in Reinheitsgebot-controlled Germany, the most stringently controlled of all the Old World brewing nations. Looking back at the weizen style in this chapter (see page 62), you can see that a German-style wheat beer is a top-fermented beer – in other words, an ale. Yet a bock, as noted in "Bock to Basics" (pages 84–87), is a lager fermented with yeasts that work at the bottom of the fermenter.

So what the heck is a weizenbock?

What appears at first a paradox of a name becomes much more understandable when you realize that the term *bock* describes strength more than fermentation. In fact, the original bocks from Einbeck were themselves likely top-fermented brews, as lager fermentation and the cold-conditioning of beer was yet to be discovered. A weizenbock, then, is simply a potent German-style wheat beer.

The first beer to be billed a weizenbock was the Schneider & Sohn's Aventinus, originally brewed in 1907. (See page 64 for more on the Schneider brewery.) It is doubtful, however, that Aventinus was the first beer to fit the weizenbock bill since strong weizens had almost certainly been brewed in Bavaria; previously they just wouldn't have been billed as such.

For people who view wheat beers as simple warm-weather refreshers, the weizenbock can come as a surprise. Generally measuring between 6% and 8% alcohol, a typical weizenbock offers a mouthful of spicy flavors and a good measure of chocolate and fruit in both the aroma and the taste, all of which make it a fairly big beer. Oddly enough, the effervescence that comes from bottle-fermentation and the natural lightness on the palate of a wheat beer also allow the weizenbock to retain some of its quenching character. To someone drinking for refreshment, this can make for quite an ominous prescription.

Nevertheless, this combination of potency and a quenching character does make the weizenbock a fine beer for combining with food. In particular, a good weizenbock will serve as a good foil for a plate of flavorful sausages and spicy sauerkraut.

Many of Bavaria's wheat beer breweries produce a weizenbock, although the beers are frequently available on only a seasonal basis. Maisel, the Franconian brewery in Bayreuth that also brews a peppery, fruity Weisse, produces a full-bodied, slightly sharp tasting Weizenbock of 7% alcohol, while their southern Bavarian neighbor, Hopf, brews a fruitier Weisser Bock of the same strength in Miesbach. Erdinger, located just outside Munich in Erding, complements their fruity Weissbier with the smooth, chocolaty Pikantus.

In North America, the weizenbock remains a much more elusive creature than in Bavaria. Maryland's most Germanic brewery, the Baltimore Brewing Company, offers a fruity, 6.9% alcohol DeGroen's Weizenbock, while the impressive, multifaceted Victory Brewing of Downington, Pennsylvania, provides a spicy Moonglow Weizenbock as a fall seasonal. Elsewhere, weizenbocks can be found as sporadic offerings from brewpubs such as Seattle, Washington's Elysian Brewing and Toronto, Ontario's Denison's Brewing.

AVENTINUS

Price: $$
Freshness & Durability: ✳ ✳
Availability: ✓ ✓

In the late 1800s, competition was fierce among
Bavarian doppelbock brewers as each tried to
grab a piece of the strong-beer pie held by the
Salvator of Munich's Paulaner brewery. In such
company, what is a poor hefeweizen brewer to
do? Why, produce the brewing world's first
wheat-based doppelbock, of course.

As noted on page 71, it is unlikely that the
Schneider Aventinus crafted in 1907 truly was
the original weizenbock. Rather, brewing histori-
ans suggest, the first bocks of Einbeck were top-
fermented beers made from barley and wheat
malt. But Aventinus was the first beer to claim
the title of weizenbock, and that fact plus its unflagging quality are certainly
enough to earn it honors as the definitive weizenbock beer.

As a hefeweizen, Aventinus possesses the spicy, refreshing qualities of
other German wheat beers. As a doppelbock-strength brew, however, the 8%
alcohol potency of Aventinus should give pause to anyone tempted to down a
few after a day in the sun. Much better to put the chocolaty, fruity spice of the
beer to good use as a complement to spiced and barbecued pork or desserts
such as chocolate spice cake. I also enjoy it as a nightcap in July or August,
when a barley wine or old ale would feel a little too heavy.

HOPS GOOD,
MORE HOPS
BETTER

As inconceivable as it may be to the hop devotees
of the modern craft-beer renaissance – "hop
heads," as they proudly call themselves – hops
are relative newcomers to the brewing process.
While their use can be traced to pre-Christian
times, the popular employment of hops in brewing dates only to some time around 800 AD, many
millennia after the first beer was brewed. Then,
they were prized for their preservative effect.

Today, hops are thought of mostly in terms
of their bittering and aroma qualities. And oddly
enough, considering that the continent's most
mainstream brands of beer show little hop
character, North America has recently become
the world capital for extremely hoppy beers.
Many brewers, particularly those of northern
California and the Pacific Northwest, prize
the high alpha acids and intense aromatics of
American-grown hops and use them to their full
advantage, often creating beers of challenging
bitterness. In this fashion, they have redefined
the way that hops can be used in brewing.

North American Pale Ale

The beer style known as pale ale is a source of no small amount of confusion for many North American beer drinkers. If it is a "pale" ale, the common question goes, then why is it so dark? And if ales are supposed to be fruity, then why is a pale ale so bitter? It just doesn't seem to make any sense.

Understandable as the confusion is, it is also easily explained. The reason the ale is called "pale," even when it most often appears dark, is that when the style was born in Britain around the end of the 1700s, most beers were even darker. So while the new pale ales were hardly as light and golden as our modern lagers, they were considered quite pale relative to the rest of the beer being consumed.

As for the bitterness of a pale ale, that is a result of the hops. And in the North American pale ale, more of those hops come into play than in any other ale style in the world, making for a strongly bitter, sometimes citrusy brew unique to the continent.

Pale ales and British-style best bitters were once the dominant beers in North America, brought to these shores by the original British settler brewers. This situation began to change toward the end of the 19th century as German brewers brought new lager-brewing techniques to the New World. They converted many ale drinkers and by the early years of the 20th century, ale brewing was well on the wane.

The popularity of ales continued to decline through the end of the 1970s, when beer production in North America was consolidated as never before in the hands of a few large brewing companies. Then came the first rumblings of the craft-beer renaissance, and soon pale ales began their resurgence, led by a small California brewery and their assertively hoppy ale.

Sierra Nevada Pale Ale soon became the catalyst behind a new generation of American pale ales. Following the Sierra lead, these beers were uniformly well hopped, with much of their character coming from domestically cultivated hops strains such as cascade and chinook. They were proudly and aggressively citric in aroma and bitter in flavor, and even if some brewers tended to over-hop or forget that there is a limit to how much bitterness a beer can handle without a corresponding increase in malt, they were for the most part welcomed by a hop-starved beer-drinking populace.

Whether all of these hops are a good thing depends on your perspective. Bitterness in beer is an acquired taste, much like the bitterness found in rapini or radicchio, the dryness of a good Bordeaux or the pungency of garlic. Once a person becomes accustomed to them, though, there is much gastronomic pleasure to be found in such intense and unyielding tastes, and hoppiness is no different. In particular, hoppy ales are fine complements to extremely spicy foods, and yet they are also versatile enough for backyard barbecues or an afternoon or evening spent down at the pub.

There are far too many fine North American pale ales brewed across the United States and into Canada today to even begin to list them all. Northern California in particular is rife with them, from the sublime Red Nectar of Arcata's Humboldt Brewing to the more challenging Red Seal Ale of Fort Bragg's North Coast Brewing. Still more fine pales can be found in the Pacific Northwest (Deschutes Brewing's Mirror Pond from Bend, Oregon, and the Pale Ale of Seattle, Washington's Pyramid Brewing), the Midwest (Burning River Pale Ale from Cleveland's Great Lakes Brewing), the East (the intimidatingly named Alpha King from Three Floyds Brewing of Hammond, Indiana) and virtually everywhere in between.

SIERRA NEVADA PALE ALE

Price: $
Freshness & Durability: ✳ ✳
Availability: ✓ ✓ ✓

A seminal beer in the short history of American craft brewing, the Sierra Nevada Pale Ale has played a pivotal role in changing the face of beer in the United States. Much as the Samuel Adams Boston Lager redefined what lagers brewed in the United States could be, so Sierra Pale altered the nature of American ales. It was not the first beer of the craft-brewing renaissance to use increased amounts of hops, but it was the most influential.

When Sierra Nevada Brewing came on the scene in 1979, beers that had significant amounts of bitterness and hop aroma were in seriously short supply in the United States. Sierra Nevada, along with other landmark breweries such as Mendocino Brewing, the Boulder Brewery and Newman's, began to change that situation almost immediately by producing beers with character, distinction and, of course, significant amounts of hops.

The now-iconic Sierra Nevada Pale Ale is given a pleasingly refreshing character through the judicious use of American-grown cascade hops and enough malt to back up the bitterness. The resulting beer is somewhat citric, even grapefruity, and sweetly floral, with a satisfyingly dry finish. It is a member of that exclusive fraternity of beers that can quench a thirst in the heat and satisfy the soul in the cold.

ST. AMBROISE PALE ALE

Price: $
Freshness & Durability: ✳ ✳
Availability: ✓ ✓ ✓

Back in the early 1970s, when most breweries were in the process of exorcising virtually all the hop character from their beers, a funny thing was happening in Quebec: big brewers were still loading their ales with hops – not the "knock your socks off" kind of hopping rates that some craft brewers employ today, but significant amounts for the time. They did this because, even back in the dark days of North American brewing, Quebecers were famous for their love of hoppy ales.

Sadly though, as hopping rates dropped even further across Canada, they also fell in Quebec, although they still remained proportionately higher. Thus, when Peter McAuslan got the idea to open a craft brewery in Montreal in 1988, the beer he wanted to brew was the beer of his youth: a nice, hoppy Quebec pale ale.

He was successful in his quest, and today the St. Ambroise Pale Ale could be considered the Sierra Nevada Pale Ale of Canada. Rusty orange in color, it has a pleasantly fruity, nutshell aroma and a full and marvelously balanced flavor blending nutty and woody hop notes with peachy and orangey fruit. A pleasure at the table with spicy food or enjoyable on its own, it is a beer that speaks not only to Quebec's brewing heritage, but to that of Canada as a whole.

Like the beer that gave it two-thirds of its moniker, pale ale, the India pale ale is a bit of a conundrum. To begin with, there is the name, which does not mean that the first India pale ale came from India, but rather that it was destined for there.

The creation of a London brewer named Hodgson, the India pale ale, or IPA as it is commonly abbreviated, was developed in the early 1800s in response to the difficulties British brewers faced in exporting beer to Commonwealth troops and other British subjects in India. As it was, the popular porters shipped in wooden casks spoiled and soured on the long journey. What was required was a beer of greater stability and durability.

Enter Geoffery Hodgson. Recognized in London as a brewer of pale ales even before those beers achieved significant popularity there, Hodgson theorized that by increasing the strength and hoppiness of his beers, he could make them travel better. It was sound thinking, since alcohol and hops both act as preservatives, and it worked.

Hodgson's idea caught on quickly, and the IPA became recognized as a style unto itself, with higher alcohol, greater bitterness and often lighter color than an ordinary pale ale. It remained a popular brew for many a year following its introduction – so popular, in fact, that poor Hodgson was soon left in the IPA dust by the very competitors he had inspired. By the middle of the 20th century, however, the India pale ale had lost its luster in the British market, and many English IPAs had become, and do remain, virtually indistinguishable from their pale ale and best bitter counterparts.

Fortunately for beer drinkers who love their hops, American craft brewers soon appeared to pick up the slack. Even before Sierra Nevada began test- brewing their now-celebrated pale ale (see page 78), Anchor Brewing of San Francisco was experimenting with a light gold, well-hopped and fairly strong seasonal IPA in 1975. That beer went on to become Liberty Ale and is now viewed by many as the vanguard of the American IPA movement.

While some brewers in the United Kingdom have rediscovered the pleasures of a true IPA, it is in the United States that the style has thrived. Normally of a pale gold to copper color, the New World IPA is characterized by a very hoppy, often grapefruity flavor and aroma and a relatively high strength of at least 5.5% alcohol by volume, often much more. It is a beer that announces its presence with a bold declaration.

The only question remaining is where the line should be drawn between pale ale and IPA. But differentiating between the two is not that simple. In hop-happy northern California, for example, what might be considered an IPA in the Southeast or Midwest would be viewed as a mere pale ale, while in the Northeast, the boundaries can change almost with every town visited. In the end, the key lies in but two constants, alcohol and hoppiness, and what those levels should be for a pale ale to become an IPA is largely a matter of regional, if not individual, choice.

As with the North American pale ale, a multitude of worthy IPAs are brewed all across the United States and even up into normally unhoppy Canada. In Vancouver, Storm Brewing delights with their "on-the-edge" Hurricane IPA, while south of the border, the Full Sail IPA from Full Sail Brewing of Hood River, Washington, serves up a tantalizing mix of peach and hop flavors. In Colorado Springs, Phantom Canyon Brewing's India Pale Ale strikes a beautiful balance between hops, malt and alcohol, while Victory Brewing's Hop Devil IPA makes the trip to Downington, Pennsylvania, well worth the effort. And in Anchor Brewing's northern California backyard, Sierra Nevada Brewing's seasonal Celebration Ale has been known to draw hop-headed admirers from across the continent, including a fellow who once flew from New York to San Francisco just to pick up a few cases!

ANCHOR LIBERTY ALE

Price: $
Freshness & Durability: ✴ ✴
Availability: ✓ ✓ ✓

It is an all-too-rare but nonetheless quite wonderful thing when a brewery is so skilled at producing great beers that almost anything they touch, of whatever style they choose, turns to liquid gold. Anchor Brewing of San Francisco, California, is one such brewery. From their roots with the eminently drinkable but complex and sophisticated Steam Beer, Anchor has led the way at virtually every step of the continental craft-brewing renaissance, with great brews such as Old Foghorn Barley Wine, their ever-changing seasonal Our Special Ale, and the wonderful Liberty.

Born as a one-off seasonal beer in 1975, Liberty became such a favorite that brewery owner Fritz Maytag was compelled to bring it back, first as a sporadic offering and then as a year-round product. One sip will tell the curious all they need to know about how it became so popular.

The whole hops that are used in the creation of Liberty Ale are evident at even the most casual of nosings, but unlike so many other hop-heavy beers, there is more to this ale than just the bitterness. Peach and apricot mix with the citric fruitiness of the hop in the aroma, a full mouthfeel starts sweet and fruity and gradually bitters through the taste, and the finish dries out with lingering, spicy hop notes. As an aperitif, beside a meal of chili-rubbed barbecued steak or by itself on a warm evening, Liberty Ale is a true delight.

BROOKLYN EAST INDIA PALE ALE

Price: $
Freshness & Durability: ✳ ✳
Availability: ✓ ✓ ✓

When the Brooklyn Brewing Company started out, they did not even have a brewery. Beginning life as a contract brewing company – contracting other breweries to produce their beers, in other words – Brooklyn nevertheless quickly built itself a strong reputation, even among the notoriously anti-contract-brewing beer aficionados of the United States.

Brooklyn Brewing built its reputation on good beer, from the original Brooklyn Lager to the Brown Ale, Monster Barley Wine and Black Chocolate Stout. Of course, now that the company has its own brewery in Brooklyn – although it does still employ contractors to make some of the Brooklyn brands – it has no further liabilities in the eyes of the beer snobs, nor should it.

Like so many of the Brooklyn brands, the EIPA is a stylistic tour de force. From the nuttiness of the aroma to the light sulfury, minerally qualities of the taste, the EIPA is truly reminiscent of a real British IPA, except, of course, that there are few such beers brewed in England these days. So the upstart colonists must lead the way, and lead they do, with a beer that would be completely at home beside a pub pie or served in a pint sleeve at the Rover's Return pub in television's *Coronation Street*.

BOCK TO BASICS

When I was growing up in Montreal, Quebec, I remember my father embarking on a beer-buying sojourn that quickly became a regular family expedition. As soon as spring hit and the scent of nature in growth began to perfume the air, off we would go to Ontario, where my dad could get the first of the season's bock from that province's Formosa Brewery.

Bocks can be like that. They are romantic beers, often associated with a season, and along with it, a seasonal ritual. Whether it is the fall or winter bock releases pursued by some breweries or the more traditional spring launch, the arrival of the bock is treated by beer aficionados as a sign of seasonal change, as important as setting clocks forward or putting away winter boots.

Three stories continually revolve around the subject of bock beer, one reasonable enough to be valid, one apocryphal and one that belongs solely to the annals of urban legend.

The urban legend, which dates back to an era in North American brewing when anything that wasn't a pale golden lager was viewed with suspicion, was known to every schoolboy who professed an oh-so-adult understanding of beer, and was even repeated by noted drinks writer Alec Waugh in the *Wine and Spirits* volume of the historic Time-Life's Foods of the World series of books. Said legend professed that, in Mr. Waugh's own words, "[bock] is made by using the sediment collected from the fermenting vats when they are cleaned in the spring of each year." It was as false as false could be.

The more believable but still somewhat dubious story involves two German brewers who were fighting over whose beer was stronger. To settle their dispute, the men decided to sit down and drink each other's beers until one of them got drunk, thereby proving the potency of the other's brew. After a time, one brewer arose from his chair and stumbled, but immediately covered his misstep by claiming that a nearby goat (*bock* in German) had bumped him and caused the stumble. Replied the other with a laugh, "The *bock* that tripped you was brewed by me."

Finally, the most accepted story behind the bock name relates to the north German town of Einbeck. Wanting to ship their beer south to the city of Munich, Einbeck brewers decided to make a stronger brew that would be less likely to spoil during the long voyage over land. The Bavarian dialect changed the pronunciation of the name of the town and the beer became first known as "Einbock beer," and eventually as "bock."

The original bocks were most likely strong wheat beers, what we would describe today as weizenbocks (see page 71). They would have been dark, as most beers were at the time, and likely very strong, closer in alcohol content to what we would describe, in modern beer parlance, as doppelbocks (see page 91). Today's bocks are slightly more benign characters.

Like the vast majority of German beer styles, bock is a bottom-fermented beer belonging to the lager family. Most are still dark of hue, although mai-bocks, literally "May-bocks," are typically pale. Strength should measure in at a minimum of 6% alcohol, and flavors are sweet without being fruity, with some spiciness and malty complexity considered an asset. They are ideal early spring beers to enjoy when there is a breath of new life in the air but also a hint of winter's lingering cold. They pair well with pork dishes, strongly flavored fish like grilled salmon and, interestingly enough, pasta and tomato sauce. (Although perhaps not so oddly; Italian restaurants are common and popular in Munich!)

Given that bottom-fermentation is not standard practice among American craft brewers, there are a surprising number of good bocks available in the United States. New Glarus Brewing of New Glarus, Wisconsin, better known for its outstanding fruit beers, also offers a chocolaty Uff-da Bock, while Saxer Brewing in Portland, Oregon, provides a trio of bocks, including a 7.2% alcohol, golden Saxer Bock. In Canada, Creemore Springs Brewing of Creemore, Ontario, leads the way with their seasonal Ur-Bock, and in Norway, breweries are almost expected to produce a bock among their brands, with the most famous internationally being that of Aass (see page 89).

Of course, Germany remains the heartland for bock, although the export market is fueled more by doppelbocks. Ayinger Brauerei, located northeast of Munich in Aying, brews a soft, spicy Maibock, while in the Bavarian capital itself, the slightly bitter Paulaner Bock and fruitier Hacker-Pschorr Bock are made by Paulaner at the same brewery. In Franconia, north of Nuremberg, the Bamberg smoked-malt brewery, Heller-Trum, brews the intense, smoky-roasty Schlenkerla UrBock.

EINBECKER UR-BOCK

Price: $$
Freshness & Durability: ✳ ✳
Availability: ✓ ✓

The slogan of the brewery reads (in German, of course): "Without Einbeck, There Would Be No Bock Beer." And the "goat" theory of the style's origin notwithstanding, the statement rings true. It should therefore come as no surprise that not one but three of the world's classic bocks are still brewed today at the Einbecker Brauhaus in this small north German town.

The Einbecker brewery is the last remaining in Einbeck, and its principals take their responsibility as keepers of the bock flame quite seriously. While a Brauheren Pilsner is also produced by Einbecker, it is the seasonal rotation of bocks that remains its true raison d'etre.

According to beer writer Michael Jackson, it is the company's owners' belief that the original bocks of Einbeck would have been well fermented by the time they reached Munich, and for this reason all three modern Einbecker bocks are styled quite dry. The pale bock, Ur-Bock Hell, is lightly malty and perfumey; the Ur-Bock Dunkel, or dark bock, is maltier but still dry-ish; and the Mai-Ur-Bock, brewed to the pale maibock style, is spicier and the most rounded of the trio. Any of the three would make a fine midafternoon restorative or a suitable complement to a simple meal of sausages, mustard and bread.

AASS BOCK

Price: $$
Freshness & Durability: ✳ ✳
Availability: ✓ ✓ ✓

If you want to market a brewery's beers in the English-speaking world and that brewery has a name like Aass, you had better be sure that you have some substance to back up the label. Fortunately, in the case of this Norwegian brewery's excellent Bock, such is very much the case.

Properly pronounced "ouse," the Aass brewery is named after the family that bought it in 1860 and, in the fourth generation of ownership, runs it still today. It is also Norway's oldest brewing company, having been originally established in 1834, and it produces several other brews in addition to the Bock, including a nutty, malty Juleøl.

The Aass Bock is a wonderfully malty but dry-tasting bock. On the nose, it offers roasty notes of dark chocolate, and while it hits the front of the tongue with some chocolaty sweetness, that taste quickly recedes under a blanket of roasty, earthy cocoa and licorice notes, with the only evidence of its 5.9% alcohol coming in the fresh and warming finish. While it is my opinion that few bocks can hold their own beside an after-dinner selection of hard and soft cheeses, the Aass is one deliciously rewarding exception.

The German word *doppel* means "double," and in the world of beer, its presence on the label is a certain indicator that the potation in your hand is a strong one. (The Belgian abbey-style dubbel [see page 129] is another strong "double" beer.) What the "double" in doppelbock does not mean, however, is that the beer has twice as much alcohol as a regular bock.

Given that a standard bock is typically about 6.5% to 7% alcohol, a doppelbock would be required to reach the stratospheric level of 13% to 14% alcohol in order to double it. And while some beers do attain such lofty heights, they are very few and far between. A typical doppelbock, on the other hand, will measure some 7% to 8% alcohol: still impressively potent, but not quite double strength.

What the "double" in doppelbock does mean is that the beer in question is a more muscular and robust version of a bock, much as a bigger best bitter is designated extra special bitter (ESB) in the U.K. and the Belgian abbey-style beers increase from single (*enkel*) to double (*dubbel*) to triple (*tripel*) and finally quadruple (*quadrupel*), although it should be noted that the Belgian brews also change style considerably as they progress up the scale.

The roots of the doppelbock can be found in the church, or, more specifically, the monasteries of the followers of St. Francis of Paula. Having arrived in Munich from Italy in the wake of the 16th-century Reformation, the Paulaners, as the monks were known, were committed to upholding the rites of the Catholic Church, including twice-a-year forty-day fasts. During these periods, food was forbidden but liquids allowed, and so the monks brewed for themselves a rich and nutritious beer to help keep body and soul together. (Although one has to wonder what "visions" might have resulted from drinking doppelbock on an empty stomach.)

Over time, word of this supremely rich bock spread among the citizenry of Munich, and secular brewers turned their hands to brewing a similar beer, almost uniformly known by the same name the monks had bestowed upon their beer: Salvator. This practice eventually fell by the wayside, but the tradition of ending the names of doppelbocks in "-ator" has prevailed world-wide, resulting in a host of interesting and occasionally amusing monikers such as Celebrator, Optimator, Terminator and even Procrastinator.

Some of the most inventive names have come from U.S. breweries, but so have many impressive doppelbocks. The Boston Beer Company loses a point for their lack of name originality but scores high for flavor with their balanced, chocolaty Samuel Adams Double Bock; Stoudt Brewing of Adamstown, Pennsylvania, gets sweet with a gently nutty Honey Double Mai-Bock; and Frederick Brewing of Frederick, Maryland, gets high marks for both name and flavor in their chocolate-cherry Blue Ridge Subliminator Doppelbock. Canadians Brick Brewing of Waterloo, Ontario, and Brasserie GMT of Montreal, Quebec, represent north-of-the-border doppelbocks with, respectively, a thick, warming Brick Bock and a faintly whiskey-ish Canon.

Quite naturally, German brewers remain responsible for some of the finest doppelbocks available, including the beer that started it all, Salvator. Others include the faintly smoky, spicy Optimator from Spaten of Munich, the massive, 12% alcohol Kulminator 28 from EKU of Kulmbach, and the raisiny, spicy Ritterbock from the Kaltenberg brewery located just outside Munich. Elsewhere in the world, Feldschlösschen of Rheinfelden, Switzerland, has seen fit to cease production of the outstanding dark chocolaty Samichlaus, although older vintages are still available and there is some hope that its brewing may resume. Moretti of Udine, Italy, offers what is arguably that country's most full-bodied brew, the malty, chocolaty La Rossa.

Most often too rich to pair with main courses, doppelbocks are at home in the dining room when chocolate hits the table, whether in the form of a Bavarian chocolate cake, dark chocolate mousse or artistically prepared truffles. They are also one of the few bottom-fermented beer styles with the character to stand up alongside a good cigar, particularly if the smoke in question is a spicy one, such as a Montecristo No. 4.

SALVATOR

Price: $$
Freshness & Durability: ✳ ✳ ✳
Availability: ✓ ✓

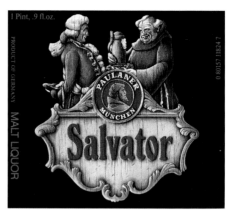

A beer to save the soul? Perhaps not, but over the years Salvator – meaning "savior" in Latin – must have turned more than a few minds toward quiet contemplation with its richly warming character.

The original doppelbock, Salvator has quite a legacy and reputation to uphold. Fortunately, it is up to the task. The three malts used in its brewing are present in abundance in both the aroma and body of this russet-colored brew, with a rich mixture of toffee, chocolate and orange brandy notes in the nose and a very full, caramely body. The finish, while drier than the body, leaves the feeling that you have just eaten rather than drunk. That the Paulaner brothers first brewed this beer as a "liquid bread" is easy to understand.

Then again, with 7.5% alcohol, this might not be the first beer I would choose if I was fasting. (Although records indicate that the first Salvators were of the same starting but higher finishing gravities, which would mean more sugars and less alcohol present in the final beer.) Better to enjoy a Salvator, I think, with a good cigar, a quiet conversation or a thick piece of dark chocolate and a much thicker book.

CELEBRATOR

Price: $$
Freshness & Durability: ✳ ✳
Availability: ✓ ✓ ✓

On more than one occasion I have heard the Celebrator referred to as "that goat beer." Take a look at the bottle and the reasoning behind the nickname becomes perfectly clear: two German "bocks" adorn its label and a third plastic one hangs from a string wrapped around the bottle neck. If nothing else, this is a beer that cries out to be noticed.

Of course, there is more reason to note the Celebrator than simply its multitude of goats. This beer, known as the Fortunator in Germany, is an excellent example of a fine German doppelbock and also one that makes me think of the way these beers were perhaps once brewed. This distinction becomes immediately visible when the beer is poured: the Celebrator is among the darkest of the doppelbocks, almost pitch black in color and reminiscent of the burnt barley malts in use before malting became the exact science it is today.

In the body, it also has a rustic quality about it. With a mocha-ish combination of coffee and chocolate notes in the flavor and a round, faintly scorched sweetness, the Celebrator is a beer that brings to mind home-cured sausages and coarse black bread. And with its dry, only mildly alcoholic finish, who is to say that it wouldn't complement such a feast superbly?

Back in 1797, in the German duchy of Franconia, a hapless vintner came face-to-face with every farmer's nightmare: he discovered his precious crop of riesling grapes had frozen solid on the vine. Resigned to the catastrophe, he pressed the fruit anyway and, in so doing, created a luscious, rich wine of exquisite character and generous alcohol. He had just discovered what the world now knows as eiswein, or ice wine.

What does this have to do with beer? Well, somewhere along the time line – perhaps earlier, perhaps later – a German brewer found himself in a similar position, except rather than frozen grapes he faced partially frozen beer. He could have taken it indoors to melt by the fire, but instead he drew off some of the unfrozen brew and discovered a sweet, strong and superbly nuanced beer. His was the first eisbock.

The secret to eisbock is that partial freezing of the beer. Because water freezes at a higher temperature than alcohol, when ice is drawn off the beer, it concentrates the remaining liquid, resulting in more intense flavors and aromas and higher strength. It is an old and respected process, and one that has little to do with the huge crop of North American "ice beers" that appeared on the market in the late 1990s. (Ice beer, as brewed by major breweries, and eisbock use ice for different purposes. In most ice beers, the partial freezing of the beer occurs either during or as close to filtration as possible and is employed primarily as a way to lend maximum "crispness" and "clarity" to the beer, or at least that was what Labatt claimed when they introduced Labatt Ice to Canada in 1993. As most major breweries ferment their beers to high levels of alcohol and dilute them to lower levels at bottling – a common practice known as high-gravity brewing – whatever concentration did occur would be undone by the reintroduction of water later on.)

Typically very high in strength – an alcohol content of 10% or more is not uncommon – eisbocks are best enjoyed as a digestif after a meal, although some pair quite nicely with chocolate desserts. The danger lies in their smoothness; bottom-fermentation tends to yield very drinkable results, even at high alcohol levels, and in the case of eisbocks, that quality could lull someone unaware of the true strength of the brew into drinking too much.

Worldwide, precious few eisbocks remain in production. The situation turned especially bleak in 1996 when Kulmbacher Reichelbräu, brewer of the Eisbock Bayrisch G'frorns, purchased the nearby EKU brewery and announced that they would continue to brew EKU's Kulminator "28" doppelbock rather than their own classic eisbock, explaining that the products were too similar to share the market. In the face of a considerable outcry from beer aficionados around the world, Reichelbräu has indicated that they might reverse their decision. But as each year passes the likelihood of that happening seems more and more remote.

The Kulminator "28" is itself frequently referred to as an eisbock by those impressed with its 12% or more alcohol, but the brewery denies that this is the case. The beer is stored at between 0°C (32°F) and −2°C (28°F) for up to nine months, and ice is reputed to form during that period, but the brewers maintain that this is not to concentrate the alcohol but merely to clarify and stabilize the beer. Similarly, brewers at Switzerland's Brauerei Hürlimann (now owned by Feldschlösschen) insist that when they were brewing the now-discontinued Samichlaus, they utilized no freezing technique to concentrate the alcohol in that 14% delight.

Since U.S. laws covering the concentration of beer through freezing are rather ambiguous, few American brewers have attempted the style, and most of the beers from that country that purport to be eisbocks are of the style in name only. In Canada, however, the laws are more straightforward; therefore, the brand first produced by Niagara Falls Brewing of Niagara Falls, Ontario, in the late 1980s, the Niagara Falls Eisbock, stands as the continental standard-bearer for the style. Other Canadian brewers have also from time to time experimented with the style, most notably Vancouver Island Brewing with their potent (10% alcohol) Christmas seasonal, Hermannator Eisbock.

NIAGARA FALLS EISBOCK

Price: $$
Freshness & Durability: ✳ ✳ ✳
Availability: ✓ ✓ ✓

Since the region's ice wines now serve as the international calling card for the Ontario wine region of Niagara, and since two of the four original principals in the Niagara Falls Brewing Company came from the wine industry, it is not surprising that eisbock was the style selected for the second beer ever brewed by the company. That was in 1989, and in the years since, Niagara Falls Eisbock has become almost as famous as Inniskillin Ice Wine, which started the other movement.

When Niagara Falls Brewing began to test-brew their Eisbock, it was in all likelihood the first time the style had ever been commercially attempted outside Germany. In deference, perhaps, to the fact that Ontario at the time had few high-strength beers on the market, the brewery elected to keep their beer's potency level at a relatively modest 8% alcohol and focused on concentrating flavors more than strength. The beer that emerged was one of remarkable complexity and elegance. And it was a huge success.

After the first Eisbock sold out in a mere two months, Niagara Falls Brewing decided to make the vintage-dated beer an annual fall event. In keeping with that mandate, each year's offering changes at least slightly; sweeter or drier, more or less chocolaty or spicy, greater or lesser presence of alcohol in the flavor. In general, though, Eisbock tends to demonstrate a modest sweetness, firm body and gentle character.

FROM THE WOOD

Imagine yourself in a bar. Now imagine that the bartender has talked you into having a pint of ale – one that is dark and maybe a tad hazy, is served at a temperature perhaps not best described as warm but certainly a mile from ice-cold, and is, by all appearances, flat!

This might not immediately conform to your idea of a fabulous pub experience, but for thousands of British ale drinkers and a growing number of beer aficionados around the globe, it is beer heaven. The beer is cask-conditioned ale, more popularly known as real ale, and after years of teetering on the edge of extinction, its future is assured.

Learning to love cask-conditioned best bitter really isn't that arduous a task, although its presentation does often come as a surprise to those unfamiliar with it. Beer from the cask is beer in its most natural state, fresh from fermentation and poured without the assistance of pressurized carbon dioxide or other gases. It is full of flavor, easy to enjoy (without the bloating sometimes caused by beers with higher carbonation) and wonderful on its own or as a complement to a meal.

Contrary to popular perception, cask-conditioned bitter, like any other real ale, is not really flat, it just looks that way in comparison to the bubbly lagers and ales produced by most large, modern breweries and, indeed, many of the smaller ones. Further, contrary to the mythology that surrounds it, no real ale is at its best when served warm; a cellar temperature of 12°C (54°F) to 13°C (55°F) is about the optimum. And while a perfectly handled cask-conditioned ale will pour bright and clear, the slight haze that from time to time appears in a pint is harmless and affects only the aesthetics of the beer.

So what is cask-conditioning all about? In simple terms, it means that after undergoing a primary fermentation and filtration at the brewery, the beer is transferred into the cask from which it will eventually be served and redosed with yeast to induce a second fermentation. After that process has been completed, finings — most often isinglass, a product processed from the swimming bladder of a sturgeon or other fish — are added to the cask to draw the spent yeast cells to the bottom of the vessel. The ale is poured either by gravity or through a hand pump, also called a beer engine, which creates a suction of sorts to propel the beer out of the cask.

While any style of ale can be made "real," the most popular is the British beer known as best bitter. Typically a copper-colored, mildly bitter and fruity ale designed for easy drinking, the cask-conditioned bitter is the national ale of England, the beer that, even if it is today outsold by ales and lagers dispensed by modern draft equipment, is most emblematic of British pub culture.

It comes as no surprise, then, that locating a cask of bitter in a pub in London, Manchester or even the countryside of Yorkshire is not a terribly difficult exercise. The challenge comes in finding one that has been properly stored, tapped and poured.

Because it is a "living thing" in the sense that the yeast are still active, cask ale requires a significant amount of care and attention from the publican. Among the most basic of handling requirements are that the cask be allowed to complete its fermentation in the pub's cellar, that the cellar be kept clean so that the beer doesn't become infected once tapped, that the draft lines be kept sanitary and the pour be skillfully managed, and that the cask be consumed within a short time, preferably no more than two or three days. Failure on any of these points can, and all too frequently does, result in off-flavors in the pint.

In England, it is pretty much de rigueur that a brewery produce a cask bitter, the ever-popular pub ale of Britain and arguably the most sociable beer style in the world. Visitors to London in August can find several hundred of them at the Great British Beer Festival, staged by the high-profile beer-consumers group the Campaign for Real Ale, popularly known as CAMRA. Dozens of other festivals run throughout the year in various locations around England, or you can put together your own mini-fest by staging a pub crawl using CAMRA's *Good Beer Guide* as your map.

Cask-conditioned bitter is increasingly available on this side of the Atlantic as well. Guelph, Ontario's Wellington County Brewery became the first modern commercial producer of cask ale in North America with the introduction of their Arkell Best Bitter back in 1985, and dozens of breweries have joined them since. One of the best New World cask bitters I have come across, the Granite Brewery's Dry-Hopped Best Bitter, is brewed in my home town of Toronto, Ontario.

BATEMANS XXXB

Price: $
Freshness & Durability: ✳
Availability: ✓ (✓ ✓ ✓ in England)

"Good Honest Ales" is the company motto of the Batemans Brewery of Wainfleet, England, and it is indeed an appropriate one. "Honest" beer is beer of good character brewed from quality ingredients and handled with care from kettle to pint, and Batemans ales, including the outstanding XXXB Bitter, certainly meet these criteria.

More than a century ago, George Bateman abandoned farming to open a brewery in a nearby town, and so the tradition behind the Batemans Brewery began. Through four generations, the company has remained under the direction of the Batemans, although a rift in the family in the mid-1980s did for a time threaten the brewery's existence. Fortunately, a love of fine beer and brewing prevailed, and today Batemans is one of the most respected and awarded independent breweries in Britain.

The XXXB is a premium bitter, darker, stronger and hoppier than its XB Bitter sibling. Yet despite its big character, it is as quenching and drinkable as any "ordinary" bitter, and twice as satisfying. Its notes of fruit and sweet malt round out an otherwise dry, leafy-hoppy body to a fine, slightly off-dry finish. It is with good reason that the XXXB has three times been judged the best of its category at the Great British Beer Festival.

MARSTON'S PEDIGREE

Price: $
Freshness & Durability: ✻
Availability: ✓ (✓ ✓ ✓ in England)

One of the eternal debates among brewers and aficionados of English ales centers around where the line should be drawn between a pale ale and a best bitter. In the case of the Marston's Pedigree, for example, some point to the brewery's location in the heart of the Burton region, which is known for its pale ales, and conclude that the beer must therefore be a pale ale rather than a bitter. Others focus upon Marston's continued use of the traditional Burton Union fermentation method, a complicated system involving shallow, square fermenters, linked oaken casks and suspended troughs that collect the yeast, and arrive at a similar conclusion. Still others simply say that it tastes like a Burton pale ale.

In the end, however, it must be admitted that there is no exact definition for one or the other. Best, then, to go with the old chestnut that declares that a pale ale is simply a best bitter put into a bottle, and since Marston's Pedigree is sold both bottled and in cask-conditioned form around England, it could be that both sides in the argument are correct.

Regardless of its name, the Pedigree is a wonderful ale with a typically Burton touch of sulfur in the aroma, a fresh, rather than off-putting, characteristic that comes from the region's water. In the body, it has a pleasingly complex mix of hops and malt, with dry-ish appley notes, a hint of smoke and a long palate-cleansing finish.

When most beer aficionados think of cask-conditioned ale, the style that jumps to mind is best bitter. The reason comes as no great revelation; best bitter is by far the choice style for cask-conditioning among British brewers and beer drinkers. A quick scan of the *Real Ale Almanac*, the British guide to cask-conditioned beers, bears this out, showing that listings for bitters outstrip those of all other ale styles by a conservative margin of at least two to one.

This popularity does not mean that cask-conditioning (see page 100) is suited only to the best bitter style. Literally any ale can be cask-conditioned, from a mild of 3% alcohol by volume to an old ale of 8%, and the fact that those beers appear less regularly on the handpumps has more to do with modern drinking habits than with any incompatibility of the style with the process. In fact, it was not that long ago, the beginning of the 19th century to be exact, that the dominant cask-conditioned beer in London was not best bitter but porter.

Predating even porter is one of today's least common and most interesting cask-conditioned ales, strong ale. In the early days of British brewing, when all beer was cask-conditioned, the dominant method of brewing was the parti-gyle system in which two or even three mashes would be made from the same grain. Since each mash would wash sugars out of the malt, the resulting worts each contained diminishing amounts of sugar and so would ferment to different levels of alcohol. The original mash, or first runnings, would be the strongest and yield the most prized and expensive beer.

While the parti-gyle system has long since become a historical curiosity, the tradition of the strong ales that resulted from those first runnings remains with us. Most frequently, these beers are available in bottled form, most often either bottled in their unfiltered state or bottle-conditioned. Occasionally, however, brewers make them available as seasonal or even regularly available cask-conditioned products. (It should be noted in discussing modern

English strong ales that the levels of alcohol involved are generally less than what would have resulted from first pass of the parti-gyle system and what would be considered strong in North America. In England, where 4% alcohol by volume best bitters are the norm, it is not uncommon for a beer of 5% alcohol to be denoted "Strong Ale" by its brewer, although neither is it entirely unheard of for an English cask ale to measure 7% alcohol or more.)

Cask-conditioning bestows upon strong ale all of the advantages it hands to best bitter. Unencumbered by excess gas or frigid temperatures, the bold, complicated flavors of a strong ale from the cask shine as brightly as do the most nuanced notes of a best bitter. In fact, because they contain more alcohol, which acts as a preservative, strong ales can actually sustain their proper flavors in an open cask longer than most bitters. Indeed, Jim Anderson, who hosts the annual springtime Real Ale Rendezvous in his home city of Philadelphia, reported that a cask of J.W. Lee's Harvest Ale, an 11.5% alcohol delight, not only lasted more than a week in its cask but actually improved over the course of the first few days.

Few cask-conditioned ales of the Lee's Harvest's significant strength are to be widely found, either within England or anywhere else. More modestly alcoholic, cask-conditioned strongs are available sporadically throughout England, such as the richly malty Victory Ale from Bateman of Wainfleet and the Badger Brewery of Dorset's softly fruity Tanglefoot. Similar brews are also being sighted with increasing frequency across North America.

While these comparatively lighter ales might not bring the evening to a restful close quite the same way as would a stronger beer, of say 8% to 9% alcohol, the best of them have the added feature of versatility: not only are they satisfying late-evening fare, but they are also fine food beers, particularly with rich stews or the Sunday roast.

KING & BARNES FESTIVE ALE

Price: $
Freshness & Durability: ✳
Availability: ✓ (✓ ✓ ✓ in England)

Many a one-off brew has become so popular that
the brewery has been inspired to make it a regular
product, and the Festive Ale certainly counts
among these. Unusually, though, English aficionados of the Festive had to
wait 30 years before they were able to sup the beer on draft.

Brewed by this independent Sussex brewery for the 1951 Festival of
Britain – the event that begat London's Royal Festival Hall – the 5% alcohol
Festive was a bottled-beer success upon its debut. Unfortunately, though, the
fortunes of the two-century-old brewery were not great at the time, and the
decision was made not to incorporate the beer into their regular stable of cask
ales. By the early 1980s, however, times had improved dramatically for British
cask-ale breweries, thanks in large part to the work of the beer consumers
organization the Campaign for Real Ale, or CAMRA. So when the new brew-
house was installed in K&B's Horsham brewery in 1981, one of the first cask
ales it brewed was the Festive.

A fruity, malty ale balanced with a good dose of English hops and a
drying, fruity finish, the Festive is a satisfying ale on its own or with beef
or pork dishes. For nonresident British ale aficionados, the Festive is also
available as a bottle-conditioned beer, as is its seasonal big brother, the robust
Christmas Ale.

FULLER'S ESB
(EXTRA SPECIAL BITTER)

Price: $
Freshness & Durability: ✳
Availability: ✓ (✓ ✓ ✓ ✓ in England)

Each year at the Great British Beer Festival, the Campaign for Real Ale, CAMRA, judges British cask beers in several different categories, including strong ale. An astonishing seven times, the ESB has been judged the best in that category, and a remarkable three times it has gone on to be crowned the Champion Beer of Britain. No wonder that the fifth edition of *The Real Ale Almanac* described the ESB as "a beer for Bacchanalia with a cupboardful of awards from CAMRA competitions."

Fuller, Smith & Turner claims that there has been a brewery operating on its Chiswick site for more than 300 years, while it has been around for slightly less than two centuries. That longevity might be seen as giving Fuller's a fair shot at the title of London's brewer, except that the folks at Young's of Wandsworth, with their 400 plus years of history, might complain.

The ESB is perhaps not Fuller's most popular beer – that title would surely rest with the lighter London Pride – but it could be the brewery's best. The huge malt character that fills the mouth and coats the palate belies the underscoring of hops that prevents the ESB from becoming cloying. Strong notes of fruit lend roundness to the flavor, and the big, leafy hop finishes the taste and, as a good beer should, leaves the drinker wanting more.

There was a time, after graduating from storage in Egyptian urns and prior to the introduction of metal kegs, when all beer was kept in wood. One can only imagine what this must have done to the beer. Woody flavors would have been unavoidable, at least in the first few fillings of the cask, and the propensity of the beer toward infection must have been significant. (Such infections, more closely controlled, now play a significant role in the flavor development of certain beer styles.)

Over time and through experimentation, brewers, distillers and vintners alike discovered better ways to control the influences of the wood in which they stored their products. One way that brewers combated wood flavor in their beers was by covering the inside of the cask with pitch, a process that not only minimized the beer's woodiness but also guarded against infection. Even so, some influence of the pitch and the wood on the taste of the beer would have been inevitable.

Since vintners and distillers of that era also used wooden casks and surely experimented with ways to control the effect of the wood on their products, it is easy to speculate that perhaps some exchange of both views and casks went on among the three groups. The Scots, for example, found that used sherry casks were perfect vessels in which to age some of their whiskeys, a practice that continues today at the Macallan and other distilleries. Did brewers likewise employ sherry- or port- or even whiskey-seasoned wood? Perhaps.

Even if they did not then, they do now. The recent craft-beer renaissance in North America has prompted many a brewer to look to the past to discover the future, and some of the more adventurous of them have decided that their futures include wood-conditioned beer.

In most cases, the furthest that brewers have gone is to wood-age potent and hoppy brews such as IPAs for short periods of time, the purpose being to contribute slight oakey or otherwise woody flavors to the beers. The most experimental of the bunch, however, have opted for casks seasoned with bourbon, Tennessee whiskey or even cabernet. For these adventures, only the biggest, fullest and most potent of beers need apply.

One of the forerunners of the cask-flavored beers came from Goose Island Brewing of Chicago, Illinois, a much-lauded brewpub that has since added an equally appreciated bottling brewery of the same name to the company profile. At the 1995 Great American Beer Festival, Goose Island turned many a head and set many a tongue to wagging with their Bourbon County Stout, a mammoth, close to 12% alcohol stout, conditioned for 100 days in a cask that previously held Jim Beam Bourbon.

The success of the oakey, slightly charred Bourbon County Stout prompted other North American brewers to experiment with wood flavorings for their beers, with diverse results. At the Denver Chophouse & Brewery in Colorado, they offer a hugely whiskey-ish oatmeal stout conditioned in Jack Daniels casks, while the beer that I helped judge the best in the Barley Wine Festival at San Francisco's Toronado bar in 1998, the ever-complex and delicious Adam from Hair of the Dog Brewing in Portland, Oregon, was given an extra jolt of flavor by time spent in a bourbon barrel. And at brewpubs across North America, adventurous brewers are lining up whiskey, port and even wine barrels to fill with their most intense brews.

SAMUEL ADAMS TRIPLE BOCK

Price: $$$
Freshness & Durability: ✳ ✳ ✳
Availability: ✓ ✓

One of the best-known cask-flavored beers in the world ironically owes its fame not to the flavors of the whiskey wood in which it is aged, but to its strength. At approximately 17.5% alcohol, the Samuel Adams Triple Bock spent five years as the strongest bottled beer in the world, until it was recently eclipsed by its younger brother, the Samuel Adams Millennium Ale, first brewed in 1999.

Despite its misleading moniker, the Triple Bock is not a bock-style beer; it isn't even bottom-fermented. It is an ale, top-fermented with a particularly hardy strain of yeast, which despite its vigor still gives out after bringing the beer to about 12% to 13% alcohol. In order to increase the strength further, maple syrup and a Champagne yeast are then added to the beer, elevating the alcohol roughly four to five more percentage points. The Triple Bock gets its final dose of strength from being aged a minimum of three months in Jack Daniels casks, absorbing some of the spirit's alcohol from the wood along the way.

The final product can scarcely be called a beer, so different is it from anything else on the market. Within its first couple of years of bottled life, the Triple Bock has the flavor and aroma of a "beer Madeira," somewhat raw and medicinal in character, with Christmas cake sweetness and notable alcohol. After a few years' storage, however, the rough notes disappear leaving more complex flavors of tropical fruit, treacle and slightly resiny pine. The 250 mL (8.5-oz) bottle is the perfect size for sharing with a loved one as a nightcap.

DON'T BE AFRAID OF THE DARK

Probably no single phrase has denied beer drinkers of more enjoyment than the simple but oft-voiced refrain, "I don't like dark beer." Part of the distrust of dark beer comes from the popular misconception that beer that is darker in color must be roasty or burnt in taste. While this is indeed true for some styles of beer, it is just as false for others. The darkness comes from the malt, as does all color in nonfruit beers. And whether that malt will yield roasty, fruity, sweet or burnt flavors all relates to how much dark malt the brewer has used and what other ingredients he or she has paired with it.

I have redeemed many a dark-beer naysayer by placing a glass of softly sweet, exquisitely crafted beer in front of them. Drink one of these beers and you, too, may find redemption.

Scotch Ale

Where would you go for a beer known as a Scotch ale? Glasgow? Edinburgh? Perhaps Aberdeen?

You could try to track down a Scotch ale in any of these cities, but you would probably find yourself going thirsty. The land in which you are most likely to find the rich texture, robust body and formidable strength of a true Scotch ale is not Scotland but Belgium!

To unravel this apparent contradiction, it is first important to understand that a Scotch ale is not simply any ale brewed in Scotland. Rather, it is a specific style of ale: bold, dark, malty and, above all else, strong. It is a powerhouse of a beer, albeit softly stated, with its average of about 8% alcohol muted by a dominantly sweet and moderately roasty character. And its greatest fans are to be found among the Belgians.

During the First World War, Scottish soldiers won many friends in Belgium with both their protective efforts and their strong and malty brews. In fact, when the Scots left the country following the war, the Belgians, themselves no strangers to strong beers, began both importing and brewing this particularly Scottish style of ale, and it quickly entered the lexicon of the Belgian beer aficionado.

In the postwar period in Scotland, however, a trend began to take hold away from the strong ales that had won the affections of the Belgians and toward softer, weaker brews. The general style stayed malty — hops do not grow well in Scotland and so have never been used extensively in Scottish ale — but in a nod to the influence of their English neighbors, who favored a weaker ale, "session beers" of 3% to 4% alcohol were finding new and increasing popularity. As time passed, it became harder and harder to locate beers of the strength and intensity that once typified Scottish brewing.

Scotland's heritage of strong, malty ales is most closely replicated today in the style of beer best known as the "wee heavy," or 80 or 90 shilling ale.

(The latter two appellations, designated as "80/-" and "90/-" in the common nomenclature, refer to an old system of taxation that varied according to the strength of the beer.) While the wee heavy's typical alcohol content of 4% to 5.5% alcohol is a far cry from that of the average Scotch ale, the malty, roasty and sweet flavor profile is not unlike that of the stronger Scottish brew of yore.

Several true Highland-brewed Scotch ales are currently produced only for export because the domestic market for them remains small. Among these are perhaps the two most famous examples: the treacly McEwan's Scotch Ale of Scottish & Newcastle and the Douglas/Gordon Highland Scotch Ale from the same brewer (see page 116). Rare, locally available Scotch ales include the roasty Belhaven 90 Shilling Strong Ale and the winy Old Jock Strong Ale from the Broughton Brewery.

Elsewhere, the Scotch ale continues to thrive. The style remains quite popular in Belgium, where several breweries make their own, sometimes loosely interpreted, versions, including the rich, fruity Scotch de Silly from the Brasserie de Silly (named for its city of residence, not its attitude toward beer) and the spicy, warming McChouffe from the Brasserie d'Achouffe in the Ardennes town of Achouffe. Other Scotch ales are imported from Scotland, either in bulk or, more conventionally, bottled.

In North America in recent years, the Scotch ale appears to have developed something of a cult following. One of the earliest New World examples of the style, a lightly fruity and chocolaty Wee Heavy of 6.4% alcohol, came from Greg Noonan's Burlington-based Vermont Pub & Brewery, while a more recent entry from the opposite coast is the more typically strong and lightly peaty Wee Heavy of Sailor Hägar's Brewing in Vancouver, British Columbia. Others of note include the the sweet, butterscotchy McAuslan Scotch Ale from McAuslan Brewing of Montreal, Quebec, the bold Samuel Adams Scotch Ale from the Boston Beer Company of Massachusetts and elsewhere, and from Broadway Brewing of Denver, Colorado, the bracing Scoch ale with the quirky, Ralph Steadman-drawn label, Road Dog Ale.

DOUGLAS SCOTCH ALE / GORDON HIGHLAND SCOTCH ALE

Price: $$
Freshness & Durability: ✳ ✳ ✳
Availability: ✓ ✓

Confusingly marketed in different countries under different names, the Douglas/Gordon is one of two fine Scotch ales produced by the Edinburgh-based brewing giant Scottish & Newcastle but unavailable in its home country. This particular beer is actually brewed in Scotland and then shipped in bulk to Belgium for final conditioning and bottling by the importer John Martin. Widely available in Belgium, it is also exported from there to many nations, including France, Italy, Canada and the United States. (In the U.S., it is labeled Gordon Highland, while in Canada, it is Douglas.)

Rich and warming at 8.5% alcohol, the Douglas/Gordon lacks the cloying character of its sister brew, McEwans Scotch, and also demonstrates significantly more complexity. A lightly roasty start opens up into a full and satisfying body of subdued fruity notes, deeper roastiness, some burnt sugar and light spice, finishing with lingering, brandylike alcohol. It makes a lovely companion beverage for a good Stilton cheese or light chocolate dessert, or can be enjoyed on its own in a snifter or thistle-shaped glass after dinner.

TRAQUAIR HOUSE ALE

Price: $$
Freshness & Durability: ✳ ✳ ✳
Availability: ✓ ✓

This is a beer with a history. The Traquair House, located in Innerleithen, Peeblesshire, is the oldest inhabited house in Scotland. It is also home to one of the finest breweries in the country.

The Traquair House is owned by the Maxwell Stuarts, a family loyal to the Jacobite cause and Bonnie Prince Charlie (Charles Edward Stuart). Traquair House was once visited by the Scottish prince as well as Mary, Queen of Scots, and according to the brewery's promotional flyer, was once a "pleasure ground for Scottish kings" in good times and "a refuge for Catholic priests" in bad. Part of its attraction, no doubt, was the manor brewery, which dates back to at least 1566.

Peter Maxwell Stuart resurrected the brewery in 1965 and passed it on to his daughter, Catherine, upon his death in 1990. In keeping with the house's heritage, the beer brewed at Traquair is faithful to Scottish brewing traditions: malty, full-bodied and strong. Its hugely complex, fruity aroma foretells the pleasures to come on the palate, where the ale shows a mix of fruity notes, hints of coffee and dark chocolate, a touch of nuttiness and a lingering, warming finish. It is an ale versatile enough to be taken with a roast beef or lamb dinner, or relished on its own as a restorative or digestif.

IMPERIAL STOUT

If an award was ever presented for the most universally misunderstood beer, it would have to go to stout. "It's heavy," people say, "and rich and thick and fattening." Or they believe that it is highly alcoholic, which is true in only some cases, such as Imperial stout, but in most instances is patently false.

Nonetheless, to the uninitiated, stout remains an intimidating thing. It is black, pitch black, and that is itself enough to scare off timid drinkers weaned on golden lagers and the like. Yet within that fearsome darkness lies an element of intrigue, and human nature being what it is, we are all drawn toward a good mystery. Arguably, it is in large part because of this peculiar combination of intimidation and attraction that stout is currently experiencing a tremendous surge in its global fortunes.

The black beer that has become the star on the world beer stage is dry Irish stout, or more specifically Guinness. But the dry stout favored in the pubs of Dublin is but one of several different varieties of stout brewed around the globe: English milk stouts, with lactic sugars added for fermentation; oyster stouts, favored companion beverage for the raw mollusks and occasionally even flavored with their liquor; sweet, bottom-fermented stouts popular in the Caribbean and beyond; extra stout, brewed roastier and fermented stronger than the pub draft; and the king of all black beers, Imperial stout.

There is no mistaking the fact that Imperial stout is the heavyweight of the stout category. Typically of 8% to 9% or greater alcohol, Imperial stouts are the gentle giants of the beer world: strong and full of flavor, true, but also silken, supple and comforting. At their best, they calm the mind and soothe the soul like a gentle breeze on a sweaty August night.

As its name implies, the Imperial stout has a connection to the Imperial court of the Russian tsar. Back in the second half of the 18th century, when stout and its predecessor, porter, were the popular beers in London, many brewers in the tough, intensely competitive market elected to expand their trade through export, one avenue for which was the Baltics. Given the long voyage ahead, however, it was necessary to increase the alcohol level of the beer so that it would survive the journey. (This necessity also gave birth to India pale ale, see page 80.)

The Imperial moniker was bestowed upon this new style of stout when the Russian tsar saw fit to award the Imperial warrant to a beer exporter by the name of Le Coq, who had earned favor in the court by donating beer to fortify the Russian soldiers wounded in Crimea. The modifier stuck, and all strong, intense and heavily roasty stout became known as Imperial.

All too few Imperial stouts remain in production in England, the land of their birth. What is still perceived by some to be the classic of the style, Courage Imperial Russian Stout, has been for years a dormant brand, and few others have arisen since its demise. Fortunately, elsewhere in Europe, some old classics have been better treated. The oily, almost minty Porter of Oy Sinebrychoff AB from Kerava, Finland, known colloquially as Koff Porter, and the more fruity Carnegie Porter from AB Pripps Brygerrier of Sundsvall, Sweden, are both of the Imperial style and are both still brewed, although at 5.5% alcohol the latter lacks the style's characteristic strength.

In North America, the Imperial stout has found renewed life. The Wellington County Brewery of Guelph, Ontario, produces a rich, mocha-ish Imperial of 8% alcohol, while on the other side of the continent, Rogue Ales of Newport, Oregon, ups the ante with its own profound, almost chewy interpretation at 11% alcohol. To the north of Rogue, Yakima Brewing of Yakima, Washington, offers a more subdued, 6% alcohol Grant's Imperial Stout, and in Kalamazoo, Michigan, the Kalamazoo Brewing Company lists the remarkable 11.5% alcohol Expedition Stout among their range of four different stouts.

SAMUEL SMITH IMPERIAL STOUT

Price: $$
Freshness & Durability: ✳ ✳ ✳
Availability: ✓ ✓

The brewing business, it sometimes seems, is a particularly ironic one. Take the case of the British Imperial stout. For decades, the agreed-upon classic of the style was the Courage Imperial Russian Stout, a brand now owned by the British brewing behemoth Scottish & Newcastle. When it was brewed, the Courage Imperial was produced not in London, where the style was born, but in the northlands at the John Smith Brewery of Tadcaster. Yet the Courage stout has not been brewed since 1993, so the mantle of the classic English Imperial has fallen to the Samuel Smith Brewery, also of Tadcaster and originally owned by – you guessed it – the brother of John Smith.

While some small stocks of the Courage black may still exist, and if properly stored they should be maturing quite nicely, the better bet at this time is the Smith Imperial. It is a delightfully complex beer of 7% alcohol with notes of coffee in the nose and burnt raisins, roasted barley and fresh fruit in the body. With its lower strength and clear glass bottle, it is not, unfortunately, likely to age as well as the more potent and intense Courage, but the Samuel Smith is nonetheless every bit its equal when it comes to a fortifying midwinter tipple or after-dinner digestif, perhaps accompanied by a piece of dark Swiss chocolate.

NORTH COAST RASPUTIN IMPERIAL RUSSIAN STOUT

Price: $
Freshness & Durability: ✳ ✳ ✳
Availability: ✓ ✓ ✓

When I first visited the North Coast Brewing Company in Fort Bragg, California, in early 1999, I was most surprised to be told that the Rasputin was at the time a mere three years old. It seemed to me as though it had been many a year since I first tasted this fabulous beer during one of my frequent forays to northern California. But a beer does not have to be old to be a classic, just great. And the Rasputin is indeed a great beer, with a fabulous balance between the fruitiness, roastiness and 9.2% alcohol, and a beautiful taste profile that flows seamlessly from the sweet start to the bitter-roasty finish. A versatile cigar beer that will neither overpower milder smokes nor be lost under the taste of stronger ones, Rasputin also makes a very enjoyable nightcap.

North Coast Brewing may be a young brewery relative to the many decades of history behind the brothers Smith, but it has made its mark. In addition to the Rasputin, the northern California craft brewery also offers a very fine, very dry Old No. 38 Stout and a fruity-hoppy Red Seal Ale, among several other impressive regular and seasonal beers.

Over the natural course of brewing history, beer styles have frequently been forgotten, ignored, mutated and reborn. It is part and parcel of the evolution of the brewing arts, and is itself testament to the vibrancy and creativity of the beer-making process through the ages.

Occasionally, one of these rebirths or mutations will develop a regional following and blossom into a new style, related to but quite different from the beer that inspired it. Such is the case for the Eastern European and Caribbean style known as, for lack of a better term, strong stout and porter.

The strong stout and porter often find themselves lumped in with Imperial stout or referred to generically as sweet stout, but they differ from other stouts and porters in two very important ways. First, they are commonly a bottom-fermented beer – in other words a lager. And second, contrary to the big, full body that distinguishes almost any other stout, a stout or porter belonging to this family will be potent but oddly thin in character. In some cases, they could almost be described as refreshing.

It would be understandable to expect that the strong and sweet stouts of the Caribbean and the similar porters of Eastern Europe might share a common lineage, but in fact, their stories differ significantly. Certainly, at the root of both lies the dry Irish stout of Arthur Guinness of Dublin, itself a descendant of the porters of early-18th-century London, but from that point onward, their paths veer away from one another quite dramatically.

The Eastern European version of the strong stout has at its roots the Imperial stout of A. Le Coq and other brewers and exporters who traded in Russia and the Baltic states in the late 1700s (see page 119 for details). Naturally enough, the style was picked up by local brewers who, depending on which English brand name they were seeking to copy, called their beer either porter or stout. (Apparently, either old porter or Imperial stout was an acceptable description for the strong, sweet beer.) As these same breweries became reliant on lager sales for their fiscal health, their stouts and porters were either discontinued or switched over to bottom-fermented beers, but the strength, sweetness and the porter name stuck.

Although there were once many more, numerous examples of strong porters remain in the brand catalogues of Eastern European breweries. Two of the best-known are the mocha-ish Okocim Porter and the more purely coffee-ish Zywiec Porter, both Polish and from, respectively, the Browar w Brzesku-Okocimiu of Okocim and the Browar Zywiec of Zywiec. From Lithuania come the somewhat medicinal Vilnius Porter from the brewery and city of the same name and the maltier Utena Porter from the Utenos Gerimai brewery of Utena, while Latvia offers the licorice-ish Aldara Porter from the Aldaris Brewery of Riga.

The Caribbean tradition of strong stout is a holdover of the colonialism of the 1800s, when breweries, notably Guinness, shipped beer to the West Indies. For the same reason that India pale ales and Imperial stouts were made strong for shipping, so was the stout and porter sent across the Atlantic. This practice firmly established the Caribbean tradition of strong, sweet stouts.

It seems odd today that stouts would be brewed in the hot island nations of the Caribbean since stout, especially sweet stout, is not exactly the most refreshing of beers. But traditions die hard in beer culture, and even though companies like Desnoes & Geddes of Kingston, Jamaica, Banks of Bridgetown, Barbados, and Georgetown, Guyana, and Carib of Champs Fleurs, Trinidad, make most of their profits through the sale of light, slightly spicy-tasting lagers, all three still also make a strong stout: Dragon Stout, Ebony and Royal Extra Stout, respectively. Of course, it doesn't hurt that Caribbean mythology sees stout as a sort of "liquid Viagra," which, according to one none-too-subtle advertising campaign, "puts it back."

Perhaps because they are not thought of as classic styles, potent and flavorful Caribbean brews and strong Eastern European porters are rarely imitated elsewhere in the world of beer. If brewers were to realize how good these beers are when enjoyed on a hot summer's night with a mild Dominican or Nicaraguan cigar, perhaps that situation would change.

DRAGON STOUT

Price: $
Freshness & Durability: ✳ ✳
Availability: ✓ ✓ ✓

Jamaican beer and Red Stripe lager are pretty much synony-
mous, particularly for those who have either visited the island
or watched actor Tom Cruise knock back bottle after bottle of
Stripe in the 1993 movie *The Firm*. But as enjoyable as cold,
light lager can be on a hot Caribbean day, it can also get fairly
boring once the sun sets. That is the time for a Dragon.

Like all of the strong, sweet stouts of the Caribbean,
Dragon Stout is a descendant of the Guinness West Indies
Porter, a strong, sugar-rich version of the famous Dublin original that was reportedly first brought to the islands by settlers
in the early 1800s. A version of that beer is still brewed by
Guinness under the banner of Foreign Extra Stout, and it is
still sold throughout the Caribbean. But in Jamaica, when you
say stout, you are talking about Dragon.

There is not a lot of complexity in a Dragon Stout, but there is a great
deal of satisfaction in its gentle 7% alcohol. (And if you believe Dragon's
overtly virile advertising, that's a double entendre.) But then again perhaps it
is precisely because overly complicated ales and hot weather don't seem to mix
well that Dragon's sweet, somewhat thin and slightly anise-like body feels so
good on a steamy August night.

SAKU PORTER

Price: $
Freshness & Durability: ✳ ✳
Availability: ✓ ✓

When the Soviet Union held sway in Eastern Europe, few people were lining up to trek behind the Iron Curtain to taste the beer. And when the Communist Bloc crumbled and many of the formerly Soviet republics became independent, fewer still wanted to hop aboard an Aeroflot jet for a Baltic beer tasting.

Then came the Estonian brewery Saku to let us know that we should have been paying closer attention. A brewery since 1820, Saku was thoroughly modernized following the declaration of Estonian independence and taken public shortly thereafter. As a result, 75 percent of the company came under the control of Baltic Beverages Holding AB, a joint company of Pripps Ringnes of Sweden (brewers of the Carnegie Porter; see page 119 for details) and OY Hartwall of Finland. The remainder of Saku is listed as belonging to "small shareholders."

The Saku Porter sold in North America is marketed as Saku Tume in Estonia. (The Estonian Porter is a Christmas brew of 7.4% alcohol, compared to the 7% of the Tume/Porter.) It has a sweet, milk chocolaty aroma and lightly spicy, cinnamony body with notes of mocha throughout. What, to my mind, separates it from the other Eastern European porters I have tried, though, is the delicacy of its sweetness, which makes it a fine beer to drink when you are just hanging out, playing pool and listening to Estonian karaoke, as I did one particularly memorable summer's eve at the Estonian Club in Toronto.

ABBEY-STYLE ALE

Once there were considerably more monastery breweries in Belgium than the six Trappist-run operations that remain today. Abbey brewing in the Middle Ages and beyond was very important to the people of the territory now known as Belgium, as it was elsewhere in Europe, and in some cases, these were the only beers available to the residents of the surrounding towns. Many of the abbey breweries ceased production when they were sacked by Napoleon early in the 19th century as he rode roughshod through Europe, while others continued to brew well into the 20th century. By one means or another, though, all monastery brewing in Belgium, save for that of the Trappists (see page 156), had ground to a halt by the middle of the 20th century.

While the monastic breweries themselves may have disappeared, however, many an abbey name lives on in Belgium today through the work of commercial brewers. Grimbergen, Affligem, Ename, Steenbrugge, Floreffe, Postel, Leffe: all are names of former or present abbeys that have been either licensed to or appropriated by modern, secular breweries. Taken together, the beers sold under these names make up the block of Belgian beers informally known as the abbey ales.

Were the monastic roots of their brand names all that these beers had in common, it would scarcely be worth mentioning them as a group. But style also comes into play when speaking of the abbey ales, and appropriately enough, the styles in question are derivative of the old brewing order followed by the abbeys.

Like other breweries of the time, the monastery breweries originally brewed two styles, or perhaps more appropriately levels, of beer. The first mashing of the grain produced a sugar-rich wort that fermented into a sweet, strong ale known as a dubbel, or double ale. This beer was most likely reserved for important visitors, fasting periods (when the monks required more nutrients from their beer) and sales at premium prices. The second mash of the same grain yielded the weaker enkel, or single ale, which would fill the day-to-day needs of both the brothers and the surrounding communities. Following the Second World War, the Westmalle Trappist monastery added to these their famed tripel, a golden ale so coveted that it quickly begat a great many secular imitations and has since joined the list of accepted abbey-ale styles.

Of the three, dubbel is by far the most common. (Enkels are scarcely brewed any more, while details of the tripel style may be found on page 141.) Chocolaty and full of rich, malty flavor, with perhaps hints of spice or fruit, the dubbel is a wonderful food beer – ironically so, since the monks drank it during their fasts. It is delightful with grilled or roasted beef or horse (the latter a common meat in Belgium) and even partners nicely with many chocolate desserts.

Among the dubbels brewed in Belgium today, the soft, lightly spicy, Interbrew-produced Leffe Brune is likely the best-known. More full-bodied interpretations come from Brouwerij Moortgat of Breendonk-Puurs (the smooth, supple Maredsous 8°), Brouwerij de Gouden Boom of Brugge (the chocolate-caramely Steenbrugge Dubbel), Van Eecke of Watou (the full and fruity Het Kapittel Dubbel) and Brasserie Ellezelloise of Ellezelles (the out-standingly complex, spicy Quintine Ambrée). Many of the Trappist breweries also produce dubbels, such as the firm, dry-ish Westmalle Dubbel, the strong, fruity Rochefort 8°, and the fragrant, spicy La Trappe Dubbel.

The lack of ancient abbeys to commemorate hasn't stopped North Ameri-can brewers from producing a few dubbels of their own. In Cooperstown, New York, Belgian beer importers Vanberg & DeWulf teamed with a few Belgian breweries to open the Ommegang Brewery, the eponymous flagship beer of which should be considered a dubbel. And out in the Rockies, the Fort Collins, Colorado-based New Belgium Brewing offers a spicy, fruity ale known simply as Abbey, while another eponymous beer is the abbey-style offering of the Brasserie Seigneuriale of Boucherville, Quebec.

FLOREFFE DUBBEL

Price: $$$
Freshness & Durability: ✳ ✳ ✳
Availability: ✓ ✓

The Brasserie Lefèbvre is not widely recognized as one of Belgium's great breweries. Most people who have heard of this Wallonian operation know it more for its multiplicity of labels than for the quality of what goes into the bottles. (It is not unusual for Lefèbvre to market the same beer under a number of different names, often one for the French-speaking south of Belgium, another for the Flemish north and yet another for export markets.) Yet many of Lefèbvre's beers are deserving of acclaim, regardless of which label they are sold under. Included in this group is the delicious Floreffe Dubbel.

I developed my initial appreciation of the Dubbel at the Taverne du Moulin d'Arenberg, a café in Rebecq, Belgium, that serves as the unofficial "brewery tap" for Lefèbvre. There, alongside a *plat national* – a special plate of meats, cheeses and vegetables assembled for the Belgian national holiday – I came to understand what had eluded me in prior tastings: this was a fabulous food beer! With its fruity front and spicy, not-too-sweet body, it was the perfect complement to the cheeses on my plate, while its medium-to-full body served it well beside the meats and mustard.

In later tastings, I further developed my appreciation of the Floreffe Dubbel and lauded its versatility not only with different foods – including chocolate! – but also as an off-dry aperitif. Indeed, this is a beer deserving of far greater recognition than it currently receives.

AFFLIGEM DUBBEL

Price: $$$
Freshness & Durability: ✷ ✷ ✷
Availability: ✓ ✓

Although the label says "Anno 1074," this name is a bit of a misrepresentation. While it is true that the Affligem abbey was indeed established on that date, the monks there ceased brewing sometime around the Second World War, and today the Affligem beers are made at the nearby De Smedt brewery.

But does it really matter? Secular or not, the De Smedt versions of the Affligem ales are distinctive enough to stand up to almost any religious beer works. And in a commercial brewery, they are well complemented by such other De Smedt brews as the Celis White (brewed under license from Austin, Texas; see page 70) and the crisp Op Ale.

The Affligem interpretation could rightly be described as a decadent dubbel, with a character at cellar temperature so sweetly textured that one is tempted to pour it on top of vanilla ice cream. (Or better still, blend the ale and ice cream together to make a richly rewarding "beershake.") The aroma comes first with fruit (tangerine, strawberry) before settling into faintly spicy chocolate, and the body follows suit with a flavorful mix of apple, orange and both milk and dark chocolate. This is perhaps the consummate dessert beer, but in a pinch I wouldn't hesitate to pair it with beef or horse stew, either.

The Dutch brewing behemoth Heineken recently purchased the De Smedt Brewery. It is to be hoped that this development will not lead to the decline of Affligem Dubbel.

DEVILS
IN DISGUISE

The role that color plays in the way we view beer should never be underestimated. While we may not always be aware of it, we view darker beers differently than lighter ones. And the most common misperception we make about them concerns strength.

Perhaps because we think that darker beers should have more "stuff" in them, we tend to expect them to be stronger. In some cases, as with bocks and abbey-style ales, this is true. But in many instances, lighter-colored beers are stronger than darker ones. Britain's lighter-colored India pale ales, which are 2% or more greater in strength than that country's ebony mild ales, are one example of this phenomenon, and the golden-to-amber styles detailed in this section spell out four more excellent instances where looks can be deceiving.

The early days of brewing have left a fabulous legacy of many beer styles, among them some of the most interesting of all. Lambic, rauchbier, spiced beer and others are all holdovers from a time when certain aspects of brewing either were not understood or were still in their technological infancy. These beers arose out of circumstance and are still made today by brewers who appreciate the unique qualities these brews bring to the modern world.

Two other such beers are the French bière de garde and the Belgian saison. The areas in which they are produced – northwestern France for the bière de garde, the southern Belgian region of Wallonia for the saison – are located only a short distance from each other, but geography is not what most closely unites these two brews. For that, one must look to the early days of farmhouse brewing.

Back when the process of fermentation was only partially comprehended, enough was understood that the farmer-brewers of the time knew that they should avoid brewing during the summer months, lest the season's plentiful yeasts and other airborne bacteria spoil the batch. Besides, the long days and strenuous work involved in running a farm left little time for brewing. Yet since that same hard work also tended to generate serious thirst, the farmer was left with a problem: how could he have beer on hand while not actually brewing? It was a tricky situation indeed.

The solution that came to the French-speaking farmers of France and Belgium was the same one their German counterparts discovered – namely, to brew beer in the spring that was strong enough to withstand a summer's storage in the cellar. For the Germans, the style arrived at became known as märzen; for the northern French and southern Belgians, the styles were bière de garde and saison.

Perhaps because Wallonia is located farther from the cold winds of the English Channel than is the northern French region of Nord-Pas-de-Calais, the saison style is more ideally suited to slaking a hot-weather thirst than is the bière de garde. Generally paler in color than their French brethren, saisons are well-hopped, spritzy beers with a powerful ability to refresh despite their typically high (5% to 8% alcohol) strength. In contrast, the bière de garde is a more malt-accented brew, of similar strength and still refreshing, but ultimately more suited to evening consumption than midday rejuvenation. Not surprisingly, given the affection for fine cheese the French and the Belgians share, the saison and bière de garde are both marvelous accompaniments to the cheese course of a meal.

Perhaps because modern French brewers enjoy much less renown than their Belgian compatriots, bière de garde is rarely brewed outside France. Within the Nord-Pas-de-Calais, however, several fine examples are still produced, including the fruity, spicy Jenlain from the Brasserie Duyck of the town of Jenlain, the perfumey Bière des Sans Culottes of Brasserie la Choulette of Hordain and the unusually refreshing, certified-organic Jade from Brasserie Castelain of Bénifontaine.

Some attempts have been made at brewing saisons in North America, with wildly varying degrees of success, but the best are still to be found in Belgium. The farm brewery Brasserie Dupont makes some of the best, including the organic Moinette and the Saison Dupont (see page 137). Brasserie de Blaugies of Dour weighs in with an unusual contribution, the Saison d'Epautre, brewed from barley and spelt, while the Brasserie de Silly, named for the town it occupies, offers the very fruity Saison de Silly.

TROIS MONTS

Price: $$$
Freshness & Durability: ✳ ✳
Availability: ✓ ✓

Two popular misconceptions surround the Brasserie St. Sylvestre and its classic bière de garde, Trois Monts. The first and most common is that St. Sylvestre is a monastic brewery; it is not, although it is located across the road from a church. The second is that Trois Monts is an ancient French bière de garde rather than the modern revivalist interpretation that it is.

Owned for three generations by the Ricour family, Brasserie St. Sylvestre is perhaps the most recognized of the Nord-Pas-de-Calais breweries, having been responsible for both the first modern bière de Mars, or "beer for the month of March," and the hugely influential Trois Monts. Oddly enough, both those beers were launched in the same year, 1985, the former created by second-generation brewer Pierre Ricour and the latter by his sons, Serge and Christophe.

Certainly one of the most complex ales northern France has to offer, Trois Monts is fragrantly fruity on the nose and offers notes of dried dates and figs in the body, along with some mild woody hop and a winy, warming finish. At 8.5% alcohol by volume, it is a potent brew and well suited to combating the damp, dreary cold that sometimes afflicts the area.

SAISON DUPONT

Price: $$$
Freshness & Durability: ✳ ✳
Availability: ✓ ✓

Southwest of Brussels, en route to the city of Tournai, lies a sleepy little town called Tourpes. It is hardly the kind of place that begs a traveler to stop, unless, that is, the traveler is aware that within Tourpes resides the finest saison brewery in the world, Brasserie Dupont.

A side from a moderately crisp pilsner, all of Dupont's brewery production is devoted to beers in the saison style, from the satisfyingly potent Avec les Bons Voeux de la Brasserie ("With the Best Wishes of the Brewery") Christmas beer to the organic Moinette. It is with the flagship Saison Dupont, however, that the brewery makes its definitive statement. A simultaneously refreshing and satisfying brew, the Saison Dupont combines a distinct hoppiness with a mild but complex fruitiness and a hint of peppery spice. On its own, with a lunch of deli meats or roasted chicken, or with cheese, it is an exceedingly fine ale.

In addition to the brewery, the modest Dupont farmhouse is also home to a bakery and fromagerie, or cheese dairy. Of the three cheeses that Dupont produces, all rather confusingly marketed under the Moinette name, I was most impressed with the very soft, exceptionally flavorful raw-milk version.

STRONG GOLDEN ALE

If there is one absolute, definitive repudiation of the myth that darker beers are always stronger than lighter-colored beers, it is to be found in the guise of the Belgian strong golden ale. Strong as an abbey-style ale yet as light in both color and taste as a Bohemian pilsner, the strong golden is a powerful argument against judging a book, or beer, by its cover.

The strong golden is a creature of the modern age. Any more than a century-and-a-half or so ago, its existence would have been a technical impossibility, as malting techniques of the time simply could not produce a malt pale enough to create a beer of the strong golden's color. (The world's first clear, golden beer was the Bohemian pilsner, first brewed in 1842.)

The names of Belgian-brewed strong goldens, and indeed many of those produced elsewhere, tend to invoke imagery of hell, the devil and sundry evil or mischievous sprites. Two explanations lie behind this practice. The first is that such monikers serve as a sort of homage to the original strong golden, Duvel, a name that in Flemish means "devil." The second and, to the beer aficionado, more important explanation concerns the way in which these impressively drinkable golden brews can creep up and surprise the drinker with their equally impressive strength.

Dry, spritzy, refreshing – such characteristics are more likely associated with a pilsner, but they equally belong to a well-made strong golden. It is not surprising that beers blessed with such attributes make such wonderful aperitif drinks, with their satisfying potency offset by their remarkably appetizing dryness. And because they are typically served cold, strong goldens invite and frequently receive comparison to the chilled fruit eaux-de-vie of Europe's winemaking countries. Given the reserved but fragrant fruitiness of many strong goldens, it is an apt parallel to draw.

Many Belgian brewers have tried their hand at imitating the original strong golden, Duvel, but success has proved elusive. In the process, however, many fine ales in their own right have been constructed, such as the spicy, 7.5% alcohol Sloeber (meaning "Joker") of the Roman brewery of Oudenaarde, the herbal and 8% alcohol Deugniet ("Rascal") of Brasserie du Bocq of Purnode, the peppery, 9% alcohol Delerium Tremens from Huyghe of Melle, and the sweetish Lucifer of Dentergem's Riva.

Committed students of the Belgian brewing arts in North America have likewise made tries at replicating the flavorful success of Duvel. Unibroue of Chambly, Quebec, brews not one but three strong goldens: the 7.7% alcohol Eau Bénite ("Holy Water"), and at 9% alcohol, both the seasonal Don de Dieu ("Gift of God") and the Fin du Monde ("End of the World"), with the last being perhaps the closest of the three to the style. In Cooperstown, New York, Moortgat and two other Belgian breweries have teamed with beer importers Vanberg & DeWulf to create the Ommegang Brewery and the 7.5% alcohol Hennepin golden ale. And in California, North Coast Brewing of Fort Bragg offers its highly spicy and 6.9% alcohol Pranqster, and Russian River joins the fray with a peppery, pearish Wentzel's Winter Warmer of 6.6% alcohol.

DUVEL

Price: $$
Freshness & Durability: ✳ ✳ ✳
Availability: ✓ ✓ ✓

"It's a real devil!" So exulted a friend of Albert Moortgat's when he tasted the initial brew of Duvel at the family-run brewery in 1923, or at least that is what legend tells us. But regardless of the validity of the tale, the claim is very much true, and that is what makes Duvel one of the most often imitated but never duplicated ales in Belgium.

The "devil" of a beer that was the source of such interest in the 1920s was not the Duvel we know today. Rather, it was a dark ale, fermented with a strain cultured from the McEwan's yeast by the famed Belgian brewing chemist Jean De Clerck. In 1965, the brewery formed an alliance with the Danish brewing company Tubourg. The relationship with this well-known lager brewer might have been the catalyst that prodded Moortgat to rethink the formulation of Duvel. By 1970, amid a growing fashion for golden pilsners, Duvel became a strong golden ale.

What makes Duvel such a remarkable strong ale is its relatively dry and delicate character. Indeed, it has as much or more in common with the famously delicate kölsch ales of Cologne, Germany, as it does with its darker, maltier Belgian peers such as Rochefort 8° or even the lighter-hued Kwak Pauwel. This, plus its perfumey nose, lightly fruity, pearish flavor and dry, lightly hoppy finish, makes Duvel an ideal aperitif as well as a fine, invigorating tonic for after work.

Although the origins of most of the classic Belgian beers have been lost, the tripel can be tracked down to its earliest days. The place was the Abdij der Trappisten, better known by the name of the village it sits beside, Westmalle, located to the north of Antwerp. The time was shortly after the end of the Second World War, and the innovation was the creation of a Trappist beer of golden color.

Founded in 1794, the Westmalle abbey began brewing some 50 years later and waited another 35 or so years before selling their beer to the villagers. Sometime around 1920, the brothers finally expanded their commercial operations and broadened the market for their dark Trappist ales, and even later still, after the end of the Second World War, made their indelible mark upon Belgian brewing history with the sale of the first golden Trappist ale.

There are several theories to explain why the brothers chose to call their beer Tripel, including the idea that the wort was of roughly three times the specific gravity of their ordinary, or "single," beer, and the theory that the name was given for the number of fermentations. The more plausible theory, however, is that the "enkel," "dubbel" and "tripel" designations are merely the Trappist way of denoting strength, much as the Bavarians have their bock and stronger doppelbock, and British brewers marked multiple Xs on the sides of casks to identify ales of increasing levels of alcohol.

Today, the tripel style is so identified with the Westmalle original that it is often forgotten outside Belgium that the designation is one of strength, and thus could conceivably be applied to any such abbey-style beer, regardless of color or flavor. This truth was made clear to me in a blind tasting of 10 beers identified by their brewers as tripels, all but one of them of Belgian origin. Save for a generally golden color and elevated level of alcohol, there was little in terms of flavor or aroma characteristics that served to unite the group.

Nevertheless, since the term "tripel" is so widely identified with the Westmalle ale, it is safe to say that most non-Belgian examples and even many Belgian brands have been more-or-less modeled after the Westmalle. They are therefore uniformly strong (between 7.5% and 9.5%), light to medium gold in color and sweet to taste. It is this sweetness, and the complexity of it, that could be said to separate the true tripel from what would more accurately be described as a strong golden ale (see page 138 for further details).

Dozens of tripels are brewed in Belgium today, although, as noted above, some of them are very different from the Westmalle original. From other Trappist breweries come the Chimay White, an unusually hoppy beer that is nonetheless identified by many as that brewery's tripel, and the fruity-spicy La Trappe Tripel from the Dutch monastery of Schaapskooi (see page 156 for more on these breweries). Of secular tripels there are a multitude: the plummy, clovey Leffe Tripel from Interbrew; the herbal Affligem Tripel from the De Smedt brewery of Opwijk; St. Bernardus Tripel, a relatively weak (7.5%) grassy, spicy brew from the Brouwerij Sint Bernardus brewery of Watou; and the floral Ename Tripel from the Roman brewery of Oudenaarde, to name but a few.

In North America and elsewhere, the proper application of the tripel beer style has provoked many a discussion and debate. Is the wonderfully complex Celis Grand Cru from the Celis Brewery of Austin, Texas, a tripel? Is the nuanced Eau Bénite best characterized as the tripel of Unibroue of Chambly, Quebec? And what about the floral but conspicuously hoppy Tripel Belgian-Style Ale of New Belgium Brewing from Fort Collins, Colorado?

Perhaps the answer is to silence the debaters with a glass of any of these fine ales and leave them to contemplate their good fortune in monastic peace.

WESTMALLE TRIPEL

Price: $$$
Freshness & Durability: ✳ ✳ ✳
Availability: ✓ ✓

What is it, exactly, that makes the Westmalle Tripel such a remarkable beer? Is it the combination of its pale, pilsner-like color and high strength? (No, Duvel and other beers offer that.) Is it that the aroma and flavor are so complex they almost defy definition? (Perhaps, but surely other beers have such complexities as well.) Is it the Trappist designation? (Hardly, there are six other Trappist-brewing monasteries.) So what, then? Perhaps it is simply a combination of these and other qualities that make the Westmalle Tripel unique among beers. Like Duvel, Aventinus and a handful of other beers, the Westmalle defines its style, and like those others, it has over the years likewise defied duplication. It is a beer that is essentially impossible to classify as anything other than what, at its essence, it is: the original tripel.

The aroma of the Westmalle is the first thing that gives the taster pause. Is that spice? Fruit? Candied pear, I think. No, orange. The diverse elements that compose the Tripel's nose are so seamlessly incorporated into the whole that it is frustratingly difficult to define them. Then comes the taste, with its undisguised strength of 9% alcohol, but also with its welcoming sweetness and almost perverse drinkability. It could almost be an aperitif, but serves wonderfully as a digestif, and is also a fine complement to any number of foods, including asparagus.

BEERS FOR
THE CELLAR

Beers that are old – not old as in past their "sell by" date, but old as in years or even decades beyond their brewing day; beers that have evolved, altered and essentially changed their character from sweet and cloying to dry, dignified, complex – these are the beers for the cellar, brews not meant for immediate consumption, but for careful and prolonged aging.

To most beer drinkers, the concept of an old beer is distasteful, and for most beers, it is. But for a slim one to two percent of brews, age is a most desirable trait. Such beers are brewed to react to time like a fine Bordeaux: at first entirely too young to drink, then more balanced but still obviously youthful, and finally mature, complicated and rewarding.

There are many reasons to sit back and enjoy a beer, but unfortunately many if not most beer drinkers today think that the experience is limited to the quenching of their thirst. Be it summer or winter, afternoon or evening, these people will inevitably select as their chosen brew an ice-cold, pale golden lager, and preferably one without an overabundance of flavor.

It is a great pity, really. Not only are these individuals missing out on the vast array of beer styles presently available, including those detailed in this book, they are also bypassing one of the truly great beer-drinking experiences of this modern age: the ritual of the barley wine.

Above all others, barley wine remains the titan of the brewing arts. It is a formidable brew, so emphatically flavorful and formidably potent that it virtually screams for cold weather, a fireplace, a comfy chair and a snifter. It is a beer for the end of the night, a digestif that soothes both stomach and soul and relaxes the body for a good night's sleep. Within the world of beer, it is, as the Brooklyn Brewing Company so aptly calls its interpretation, a Monster.

Born in Britain, the term *barley wine* was originally meant to convey the fact that the brew in question was a beer with the alcoholic strength of a wine. Although the style name was reportedly in use as early as the 18th century, the first recorded evidence of a barley wine dates from 1903, when the British brewer Bass launched their No. 1 Barley Wine. (In case anyone missed the wine reference, Bass pointed out on the label that its beer had "the character of a rare wine.") Over time, the "wine strength" element became less important and the term *barley wine* came to be applied to the most formidable efforts of a brewery. Simply put, whatever was strongest was the barley wine.

In the 1980s, just as the barley wine was losing popularity in the United Kingdom and appeared in danger of fading away entirely, craft brewers in the United States latched onto the style and proceeded to make it their own. Turning their backs on such relatively weak (a mere 7.2% alcohol by volume) but well-regarded British barley wines such as Young's Old Nick, California brewers like Anchor and, later, Sierra Nevada produced immense beers with alcohol contents closer to 10%, huge malt characters and impressive amounts of hops. Simply, the U.S. brewers took everything that the Brits were doing and multiplied. By how much was up to the individual brewer.

This is not to say that the British completely abandoned the barley wine style, just that there were fewer and fewer brewed there that could compare in strength and formidability to the new generation of American barley wines. Among those that did survive are the perfumey, fruity Golden Pride from Fullers of London, which must certainly be considered the modern standard for English barley wines, and the delightfully named Bishop's Tipple, from Gibbs Mew of Wiltshire.

In the United States, the barley wine became the pride and joy of many a brewer. From the Anchor original, the style spread until barley wines could be found in almost every corner of the land. By the late 1990s, hundreds were in at least seasonal production, including the rewarding Adam of the tiny Hair of the Dog Brewing in Portland, Oregon, the big and malty Monster of New York's Brooklyn Brewery, the resolutely hoppy Millennium of Ashburn, Virginia's Old Dominion Brewing, the portlike Roundhouse from Wynkoop Brewing of Denver, Colorado, the chocolaty Old Woolly from Big Time Brewing of Seattle, Washington, and the mapley Old Horizontal of Victory Brewing of Downington, Pennsylvania. Even normally conservative Canadian brewers got into the act, as with Edmonton, Alberta's Alley Kat Brewing and their rich Old Deuteronomy.

OLD FOGHORN

Price: $$
Freshness & Durability: ✳ ✳ ✳
Availability: ✓ ✓

As much as Anchor Brewing took a chance when they introduced Liberty Ale in 1975 (see page 82), that effort was but a lark when compared to the audacity necessary for this brewery to launch a barley wine in the same year. They were not even allowed to get the name right, as the authorities of the day ruled that the word *wine*, even when attached to a beer, might mislead customers. Thus the Californian tradition of "barleywine style ale" was born.

The original Foghorn was, by reports, a sweet, pale barley wine of formidable strength and generous character. Anchor packaged it in six-ounce "nip" bottles, so as to emphasize the fact that it was a prodigiously alcoholic brew, and kegged only a very small amount of it. Perhaps surprisingly, considering that there were few beers available at the time with significant malt character and strength, Old Foghorn was a hit, although it still took another decade before the brewery added it to their stable of regular brands.

Today's Old Foghorn still offers an enormously malty and intensely satisfying character. Along with a mellow, warming fruitiness, it carries more than just a hint of spice and a relatively dry, brandy-ish finish. At a reported 8.7% alcohol by volume, it is hardly the strongest of the New World barley wines, but it is without question one of the best.

BIGFOOT

Price: $$$
Freshness & Durability: * * * *
Availability: ✓ ✓

BREWED & BOTTLED BY SIERRA NEVADA BREWING CO., CHICO, CA

A few years after Anchor led the renaissance of hoppy beers with Liberty Ale, Sierra Nevada opened with their own now-landmark bitter ale, Sierra Nevada Pale Ale (see page 78). Likewise, Sierra also followed Anchor into the barley wine field, except that whereas Anchor put their emphasis on a malty, spicy, warming brew, Sierra stuck with their strength: hops.

The owners of Sierra Nevada Brewing chose well when they selected Bigfoot as the name of their barley wine. For like its namesake, the mysterious and perhaps mythical Sasquatch, Bigfoot barley wine is an enormous creature of substantial strength and imposing presence. And also like the other Bigfoot, the beer quickly became the stuff of legend.

To this day, Sierra Nevada controls the amount of Bigfoot sold beyond the California border, recognizing that although their beers are distributed nationally, their first obligation is to their home state. Such relative scarcity is a shame, although it does contribute to the beer's renown. It means that fewer non-Californians will be able to experience the depth of flavor of Bigfoot; the way the malt gently holds the hop bitterness in place, the way the alcohol contributes to the mouth-filling silkiness of the beer, and the way all of the parts come together to make one marvelous, if massive, nightcap.

OLD CRUSTACEAN

Price: $$
Freshness & Durability: ✳ ✳ ✳ ✳
Availability: ✓ ✓

Along with Old Foghorn and Bigfoot, Old Crustacean forms the "holy trinity" of American barley wines. But whereas stylistically Foghorn is excessive in malt and Bigfoot excessive in hops, Old Crustacean has the distinction of being excessive in just about everything.

Brewed by Rogue Ales of Newport, Oregon, a brewery known for innovative and, yes, excessive beers, Old Crustacean is a massive beer that varies slightly in its excess from year to year. The 1996 edition, for example, boasted a starting gravity of 26° Plato (a measure of the amount of fermentable sugar in the wort; a basic North American pale ale will come in at about 13°), 120 International Bittering Units (a standard measure of bitterness; that same pale ale might come in at about 40 IBU) and an impressive 50 kg (112 lb) of hops per 30 barrel batch (the pale ale might have a quarter as much). You don't even have to understand exactly what those numbers indicate to know that they mean Crustacean is one enormous beer!

Known by the unfortunate sobriquet of "Crusty," Old Crustacean is a beer best enjoyed after a few years of cellar time. At that point, the hops will be better blended with the malt, the alcohol less imposing and the full and rich fruity flavors of the beer more completely developed. Then it is ready to be sipped by the fire on a cold winter's day and be fully appreciated.

Once upon a time, the distinction that made an old ale worthy of its title was a simple and obvious one: it was old. Not old in the sense that the beer had been left to go stale or the retailer had been unable to move it, of course, but intentionally aged by the brewery prior to release. This cellaring was a carefully measured step decided upon by the brewer prior to the ale's brewing and used to allow the beer to develop a complex, rounded character. They were, by all reports, highly prized beers.

Today, old ales are still highly prized, but their aging is more often than not the responsibility of the retailer or consumer rather than the brewer. With the constant pressures under which modern breweries operate, it is difficult for brewery managers to find the time, space and patience to carefully age their old ales. Instead, these beers are bottled (unfiltered, so that the yeast sediment can protect the ale during aging), often marked with a vintage date on their labels, and sold in their youth. (In England, it is possible to find old ales on draft, but typically these are "mature" or even "teenaged" brews rather than truly old ales. These beers, aged for as little as a month or two, are old only in the sense that they have richly malty, often molasses-ish characters. With alcohol levels in the 4.5% to 5.5% range, it is almost certain that "old ales" of this sort would spoil if cellared for any significant amount of time.)

It is therefore up to the beer aficionado to decide how long to age old ales. Some drinkers will prefer these beers in their heavily malty youth, when the normally considerable alcohol level of 6.5% or more, ofttimes much more, will lie muted beneath the intense sweetness of fruity, treacly brew. Others will enjoy them after a year or two in the cellar, allowing the sugars to evolve a bit into a more complex blend of flavors and letting the alcohol become more fully integrated into the taste. And still others, including myself, will push the envelope and see how long these ales will hold up, wanting to experience the remarkable complexity that distinguishes a beer whose age is measured in years or even decades rather than months.

With such patience required of the consumer, it is fitting that old ales are the ideal beers for quiet, contemplative times. All strong beers are sipping beers, but there is something about an old ale more than any other brew that inspires reflective thought.

Several classic old ales are still brewed in England, along with many others in the "younger" old ale style. Treading the line between the two is the intensely malty, 5.7% alcohol Old Peculier from the Theakston brewery of Masham, Yorkshire, now owned by the national brewing group Scottish & Newcastle. With more of a proclivity toward the cellar are the chocolaty, peppery, 6.3% alcohol 1845 Ale and the stronger Vintage Ale from London's Fuller's and the famed Gale's Prize Old Ale, a delightful, 9% alcohol brew from George Gale & Co. of Portsmouth.

Elsewhere, Brasserie Dubuisson of Pipaix, Belgium, brews the 12% alcohol Bush (called Scaldis in the United States), which has been called a Belgian barley wine but which I liken more to a Belgian old ale, and Traquair of Peeblesshire, Scotland, offers the anise-ish Jacobite Ale, an old ale spiced with coriander. In the United States, where the lines between old ale, barley wine and festive beers are increasingly blurred, it can be hard to pinpoint legitimate old ales. But certainly the roundly malty Hibernation Ale of Denver, Colorado's Great Divide Brewing would qualify, as would the chocolaty Wizard's Winter Ale of Syracuse, New York's Middle Ages Brewing and Kalamazoo Brewing's almost chewy Third Coast Old Ale from Kalamazoo, Michigan.

J.W. Lee's Harvest Ale

Price: $$$
Freshness & Durability: ✳ ✳ ✳ ✳
Availability: ✓

I sampled this superb ale immediately after I had finished judging the six finalists at the annual Barley Wine Fest at San Francisco's Toronado bar. I was seated at a table with the brewer of that year's champion beer when a bottle of 10-year-old Lee's was presented to our group as a gift and divided among the five people present. After taking a taste, I turned to the winning brewer and half-jokingly said that we would have to rescind his prize and award it instead to the Lee's. He cocked his head, took a sip and, recognizing the astounding depth and complexity of the beer before him, nodded solemnly.

Of course, we didn't actually rescind the first-place award, but the fact that the remarkable qualities of the Lee's were able to cut through the lingering intensity of a half-dozen excellent barley wines speaks volumes for this ale's inherent qualities. Brewed each season from the year's first barley maltings and hop harvest, Lee's Harvest Ale is aged for a couple of months by the brewery and released each November with a vintage date marking the year of its brewing on the label.

From its richly fruity aroma to its plentiful supply of malt and hops on the palate, Lee's Harvest would fare extremely well in the cellar. The fruit matures and mixes with the initially sharp hoppiness and 11.5% alcohol to develop into a seamlessly balanced and rounded ale. It is particularly beautiful at 10 years of age.

THOMAS HARDY'S ALE

Price: $$$
Freshness & Durability: ✳ ✳ ✳ ✳
Availability: ✓ ✓

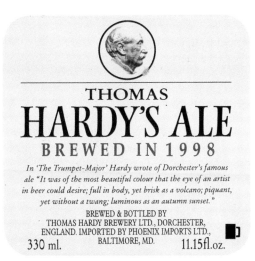

There is perhaps no beer in the world more famous for its cellar potential than the Thomas Hardy's. In 1994, I was fortunate enough to be invited to a vertical tasting of this remarkable ale that included the original edition of this ale brewed in 1968. It was wonderful; rich and astoundingly complex, with aroma notes of crème brûlée, bitter chocolate and tanned leather, and nuances of flavor that included vintage port, dried black currant and bitter chocolate. Most of the other aged bottles we opened that night were similarly, if not quite as dramatically, glorious.

The phrase most often evoked in connection with the Hardy's Ale is "brisk as a volcano; piquant, yet without twang; free from streakiness of taste." This is not a famed review of the ale but Hardy's own words, used in *The Trumpet Major* to describe a celebrated Dorset beer. These words must have echoed in the back of the brewer's head, however, when the original Thomas Hardy's Ale was produced by the brewery then known as Eldrige, Pope, as a one-off creation for the Thomas Hardy Society.

But you cannot keep a good ale down, and calls for a repeat brewing of the fine beer soon followed. Today, more than three decades later, the ale stays true to form. My preference is for at least five years of cellar time behind each bottle – long enough for the complexities of the Hardy's to develop more fully.

To many modern beer consumers, it comes as a surprise to learn that the church has long been involved in the brewing industry. In fact, in certain areas of the world at certain times, monastery breweries had a virtual monopoly on the production and sale of beer. Their saintly brews would fulfill the needs of the surrounding towns, provide hospitality to visitors and guests, and sustain the monks during times of religious fasting.

Today brewing is a much more secular pursuit. Even so, there still exist a handful of monastic breweries scattered across Europe, including a few in Germany and Austria and, most famous of them all, the Trappist breweries of Belgium and the Netherlands.

Founded in Normandy as the Cisterian Order of the Most Strict Observance, this order of monks eventually changed the name to that of their original monastery, La Trappe, and became known as Trappists. During the French Revolution and beyond, the turmoil of the time pushed them eastward into Belgium and the Netherlands, where they either built new monasteries or revived existing ones. Within a short time six of these monasteries began brewing: Orval (Abbaye Notre Dame d'Orval), Rochefort (Abbaye Notre Dame de Saint-Rémy), Chimay (Abbaye Notre Dame de Scourmont), West-vleteren (St. Sixtus-Abdij), Westmalle (Abdij der Trappisten), all of Belgium, and Schaapskooi (Abdij Onze-Lieve-Vrouw van Koningshoeven) of the Netherlands. Very recently, these six have been joined by another Belgian, Achel (St. Benedictus-Abdij), although as yet their beers are available only at the abbey restaurant.

As Trappist monks, the brothers of the abbeys are required to be self-sustaining. The monasteries make and sell goods such as cheese, bread, other comestibles and dry goods. Beer was not always brewed for retail, and even today some of the abbeys, such as Westvleteren, are reluctant commercial brewers.

Because of their common monastic roots, there is a temptation to group all Trappist beers under a single stylistic banner. While understandable, this practice is also misguided, as each abbey has over time developed a distinct style. For this reason, it is more useful to think of the Trappist label as a form of *appellation controllée* rather than as a style unto itself.

If a bond besides religion unites the Trappist beers, it is potency. The best-known beers from each of the original six monasteries are all of significant strength, at least 6.2% alcohol, and some, such as the Rochefort 10° and the Westvleteren 12, make it to 11% alcohol. Even that generalization falls apart, though, when the "table beer" of Westvleteren, the green-capped Westvleteren 4, and the new 5% alcohol blonde ale of Achel are considered.

In the most general of terms, the ales of Chimay, Westvleteren, Rochefort and Schaapskooi tend to be dark, highly malt-accented beers of great character. The single product of Orval, on the other hand, is dry-hopped to a crisp, slightly minerally flavor, while the Westmalle Tripel, that monastery's most famous beer, is golden, complexly fruity and, for a beer of such prodigious strength, surprisingly quenching (see page 143 for more details).

ORVAL

Price: $$$
Freshness & Durability: ✳ ✳ ✳
Availability: ✓ ✓

Of all the Trappists, Orval is an anomaly. To begin with, it is the only beer that the Abbaye Notre Dame d'Orval brews for sale, as opposed to the multiple labels produced by the other monasteries. Then there is its hybrid Anglo-Belg character, which sets it apart from the rest.

The English element of Orval was put in place by the second brewer at the secularly run brewery. The first brewer, a German, had already established the ale's unusually hoppy character. This second gent – a Belgian with a knowledge of British brewing ways – introduced the concept of dry-hopping, whereby hops are added to the beer between its first and second fermentation. Including the bottle-fermentation, the ale undergoes three distinct ferments, including one that involves *Brettanomyces*, or the same sort of wild yeast that ferments lambics, albeit carefully controlled in this instance.

The dry-hopping of Orval produces a beer that is at once quenching and appetizing when young, and more developed and almost sherrylike after five years. I like the ale as much in its youth, when the fierce dryness of the hop is in full force and the *Brett* culture is at its most uncontrolled, as later, when the sugars have taken hold and developed the flavors of Orval into a more complete, complicated whole.

ROCHEFORT 8°

Price: $$$
Freshness & Durability: ✳ ✳ ✳ ✳
Availability: ✓

Along with Westvleteran and, due to its relative youth, Achel, Rochefort is for many one of the forgotten Trappists. With Chimay and La Trappe scoring the honors as the most highly publicized Trappists, and Orval and Westmalle coming in a close second, Rochefort, Westvleteren and Achel are often neglected. But then again, the monasteries may want it that way.

Of the "forgotten Trappists," Rochefort is the most accessible, if only in terms of its availability. The monks at Rochefort are notoriously secretive, and visits to the abbey brewery are rare. Hardly surprising then that the brothers are not exactly budding brewing capitalists. Unlike the business-savvy monks at Chimay and La Trappe, those at Rochefort sell their beer outside Belgium only through several intermediaries.

And thank heaven for those intermediaries, because without them, beer aficionados the world over would be denied the rich and remarkably malty tastes of not only the splendidly flavorful Rochefort 6° and 10° but also the positively awe-inspiring 8°. British beer writer Tim Webb describes the 10° as "a dark, warming, cosmic meltdown of a forcefully contemplative brew." Often overlooked in favor of its stronger 11.2% alcohol brother, the Rochefort 8° is a stunning example of balance and complexity in beer. Sublimely spicy, richly chocolaty, subtly fruity, the 8° is a superb beer for enjoying with Belgian or any other quality chocolate, and an equally fine brew for in front of the fireplace on a blustery winter's day.

LA TRAPPE QUADRUPEL

Price: $$$
Freshness & Durability: ✳ ✳ ✳
Availability: ✓ ✓

Until the brothers at Schaapskooi decided that it should not be so, the highest degree of Trappist ale was a tripel. This is not to say that Schaapskooi is an abbey-come-lately – it was established as a brewery more than a century ago – however, the Quadrupel beer itself has been brewed only since 1992. And in that short time it has made a significant impact on the way Trappist beers are viewed around the globe.

In an interesting turn of events, the brewery at Schaapskooi was established to finance the construction of the monastery at Koningshoeven rather than having been added to the monastery, as was usually the case. It was successful, and today the La Trappe ales are recognized in markets around the world, trailing only Chimay in their Trappist brand recognition.

Four beers are brewed at Schaapskooi: a single (the lightly peppery Enkel), a double (the fruity Dubbel), a triple (the spicy-hoppy Tripel) and the Quadrupel. In its youth, which is to say within the first year, the Quadrupel drinks as a strong, sparkling abbey ale, with a sweet, spicy flavor but without the complexity of its similarly potent Trappist brethren. As it ages, however, the Quadrupel really hits its stride. While it is as yet too early to determine how it will fare over a decade or two, preliminary indications are that it will mellow in its spice and develop the fruit to a drier, much more satisfying degree. Certainly a beer well worth the wait!

NOT YOUR
AVERAGE BREW

When most beer aficionados think of an uncon-
ventional brew, what comes to mind is a beer with
something added, be it fruit, spice or herb. But
many of the most unusual and delicious beers
benefit not from the addition of flavorings, but
from a different treatment of the traditional
ingredients or the careful substitution of other,
parallel components.

In many ways, the beers produced by these
methods are the most surprising of all beers.
Who would expect, for example, a smokiness
in their beer? Or the taste of rye bread or Islay
whiskey? The answer is those beer aficionados
who are familiar with these brews.

Imagine yourself on a stroll through the German city of Bamberg, located in the northern Bavarian district of Franconia, directly north of Nürnberg. The scenery is that of a uniquely preserved slice of history, so perfectly unchanged from its thousand-year-old roots that the entire city has been placed on the UNESCO (United Nations Educational, Scientific and Cultural Organization) list of global cultural landmarks. Over here is a fine example of Gothic architecture; there, a masterpiece of Renaissance design; across the river, a Baroque chapel; all set in context by the imposing spires of the cathedral towering above all else in the city.

So your wandering continues as you take in the rich architectural tapestry that surrounds you. Then you stop, nostrils and curiosity piqued by the enticing aroma of brewing and what else? Smoke?

Indeed, it is smoke, and in it resides the secret of the city and the region. Because besides being a charming and important historic site, Bamberg is also the world center for a unique style of brewing, one that yields a beer blessed with some of the most unusual flavors found within the world of beer. That beer is the German smoked malt beer known as rauchbier.

To those who regularly prowl the fringes of beer styles, rauchbier is a treasured remnant of brewing days gone by, a living testament to the way beer was once made. Like Belgium's famed lambics, it speaks of a much earlier time of brewing when the science of beer was in its infancy and brewers often had to rely as much on instinct and observation as knowledge and experience. In this, it is a monument to beer's history.

The secret to rauchbier is that all or a portion of the barley malt is smoked over a wood fire prior to brewing, in the same fashion that all brewing malt was prepared prior to the Industrial Age. The resulting beer will be mildly to heavily smoky in aroma and taste, depending on how much of the smoked malt is used. For most people, the specialty beer of Bamberg is a love-it-or-hate-it proposition. Oddly, the majority of Germans residing outside of the Bamberg region fall into the hate-it category, and so one of the saving graces of the style has been its popularity in export markets.

One of the export markets in which rauchbier has had particular success is North America, where a pair of Bamberg rauchbiers, Kaiserdom and Schlenkerla, sell well as imports. And as with so many other beer styles, that success has spurred on dozens of imitators.

One of the most prolific and capable proponents of smoked malt brewing in North America is John Maier. When he worked at the Alaskan Brewing Company in Juneau, Maier formulated the potently smoky, slightly peachy Alaskan Smoked Porter, which, while hardly the brewery's best seller, brought Alaskan Brewing generous acclaim in the lower 48. Later, as brewer for Rogue Ales of Newport, Oregon, Maier came up with a second smoked malt ale, this one slightly lighter in smokiness and of perhaps marginally greater complexity, known simply as Rogue Smoke. Another North American smoked beer that has impressed – this one having nothing to do with John Maier – is the delightfully phenolic DeGroen's Rauchbock of Maryland's Baltimore Brewing Company.

Still, Bamberg remains the place to visit for those with a yen for smoky pleasures, including both rauchbier and the smoked sausage with which it partners perfectly. In addition to the great Schlenkerla and the export-only Kaiserdom Rauchbier, the city boasts the lager of Griefenklau, at most only faintly phenolic, and the marvelously enjoyable and intensely drinkable smoked malt lager from Spezial, a brewery-pub that also offers affordable accommodation in seven modest but comfortable guest rooms.

AECHT SCHLENKERLA MÄRZEN

Price: $$
Freshness & Durability: ∗
Availability: ✓ ✓

The brewery that produces the world's most celebrated rauchbier sits on a hill just outside the main town area of Bamberg. Yet most rauchbier pilgrims will not see even the outside of Brauerei Heller-Trum. For them, the ultimate destination is the place where you can actually drink the beer, the Schlenkerla tavern near the banks of the Regnitz River in the heart of Bamberg.

Once home to the brewery itself, the tavern now acts as the "brewery tap" and is considered to be the single most important spot for rauchbier in the world, and with good reason. In addition to the smoky, slightly oily Schlenkerla Märzen, the tavern also serves a smoky-clovey rauchweiss, or smoked malt wheat beer, and an astonishingly delicious, rich and roasty smoked malt UrBock. The Märzen is available in bottled form around the world, but to taste the Weiss or the UrBock, you must travel to Bamberg.

The classic, though, is the Märzen, an almost meaty brew with smoky aromatics throughout and a big, smoky, faintly woody flavor with just a hint of licorice. There is little better as a complement to smoked sausage, smoked deli meats or even a hamburger grilled over charcoal.

Alaskan Smoked Porter

Price: $
Freshness & Durability: * * *
Availability: ✓ ✓ ✓

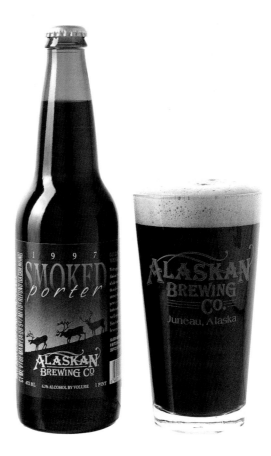

Strange things happen in the brewing world, and sometimes great beers emerge in the aftermath. Such was the case in 1988 when a plate of fish inspired the Alaskan Brewing Company of Juneau to create North America's most famous smoked malt beer.

The story goes that the brewery owners, Geoff and Marci Larson, were shooting the breeze with some of their employees over plates of smoked salmon when the conversation turned to the way that barley malt used to be kilned over wood fires. Intrigued by the possibilities inherent in this practice, the Larsons and their brewer, John Maier, made arrangements for the fish smokery across the road to smoke some malt for them, and pretty soon the Smoked Porter was born.

Extremely well-balanced, with a dominant smokiness that also complements the beer's plentiful fruity and woody notes, the Smoked Porter is a marvelous beer for spring or fall barbecuing, when cooler temperatures call for a beer with a moderate to big body. And because it has a peachy fruitiness lurking just beneath its smoky character, it pairs beautifully with virtually anything basted with barbecue sauce.

In North America, we have become so used to the idea that barley is the main
ingredient in beer that we jokingly refer to a brew as a "barley sandwich," even
if the beer in question is a major-brewery product brewed from 30% or more
rice or other alternative grain. True, the vast majority of the beers have
malted barley as the primary source of fermentable sugars, but in the past,
and in some places still, it was not at all unusual for the base of the local beer
to be something other than barley malt. Tutankhamen had his Emmer wheat
(see page 60 for details), some African breweries still use sorghum in their
traditional beers, settlers in North America added spruce to their brews for
fermentable sugars and flavor, and the Japanese can lay claim to the world's
most popular alternative grain beer, sake. In the case of the Finns, the grain of
choice for their indigenous brew, sahti, is rye, augmented by and flavored with
barley, some oats and juniper.

Once made only by farmer-brewers, sahti has become such a part of
Finnish culture that it is now produced commercially. As rye-bread enthusi-
asts might presume, the sahti is spicy, oily and almost chewy in taste. The
juniper then adds its flavor, and the top-fermenting yeast pack in an extra
fruitiness. The best-known commercial example is Lammin Sahti, potent at
8% to 8.5% alcohol and packaged in the kind of three-liter (three-quart) boxes
familiar to purchasers of bulk wines.

But Finland and its neighboring Baltic states are not the only places
where rye is used in brewing. In Germany, the Thurn und Taxis brewery
generated new brewing interest in the spicy grain with their Roggen, and
North American craft breweries were quick to pick up the ball and run with it.
At one point, numerous examples of rye beer were being produced across the
continent, and although some of those have since fallen by the wayside, others
remain, including the unfiltered Redhook Rye from Redhook Ales of Wood-
inville, Washington, and Portsmouth, New Hampshire, and the lightly spicy

and refreshing Magpie Rye Ale of the Big Rock Brewery of Calgary, Alberta.

Another popular barley supplement, oats, has been used for years to lend body and smoothness to stouts. Some excellent popular versions include the smooth and slightly minerally Samuel Smith Oatmeal Stout from Tadcaster, England, and from North America, Montreal, Quebec's richly rewarding St. Ambroise Oatmeal Stout (sold under the McAuslan name in the United States) and the almost dessertlike Barney Flats Oatmeal Stout from Anderson Valley Brewing in Booneville, California.

A Johnny-come-lately in the alternative-grain department is hemp, and it has been embraced by many a brewery in the wake of the success it has brought to Frederick Brewing of Frederick, Maryland. Used today to make everything from salad oils to clothing, hemp has also found a home in modern brewing kettles, although it is used less as a fermentable sugar than as a hop supplement. Some examples come from Bowen Island Brewing of Vancouver, British Columbia (the slightly ropey Hemp Cream Ale), Humboldt Brewery of Arcata, California (the spicy, perfumey Humboldt Hemp) and the Lexington Brewing Company of Lexington, Kentucky (the soft and herbal Kentucky Hemp Beer).

More obscure brewing grains have also found their way into beers over the generations, and many of them are either still popularly used or have experienced a recent comeback. Buckwheat, for example, is being used by a growing number of breweries, including Montreal, Quebec's Cheval Blanc Brewery in their intriguingly spicy Coup de Grisou (sold as Apocalypse in the United States), and Brasserie Silenrieux from Namur, Belgium, in their citrusy, herbal Sara. Belgian and Quebec brewers also lead the charge in the use of spelt as a brewing grain, with both the Brasserie de Blaugies of Dour, Belgium (Saison d'Epautre), and Les Bières de la Nouvelle-France of St. Paulin, Quebec (Blonde d'Epautre), making use of it.

THURN UND TAXIS ROGGEN

Price: $$
Freshness & Durability: *
Availability: ✓ ✓ (but in danger of discontinuation)

Considering Germany's centuries of brewing history, the Roggen, which was first brewed in 1988, is a very recent arrival. Modern brewers surmised that their predecessors in that region must at one point in time have used rye in the creation of their beers. Their challenge was to make one that remained true to that largely theoretical legacy and yet still commanded a place in the modern brewing world. That challenge was met.

The aroma of the Roggen has just a hint of the cloviness of a hefeweizen, interestingly enough since wheat beers are produced by the same brewery. But the dominant aromatics are those of a rustic rye bread, which makes the Montrealer in me immediately start dreaming of smoked meat sandwiches at Schwartz's Deli. The flavor follows suit, with a pleasing spiciness and slightly chewy character; now I'm really ready for that sandwich, and the kosher dill that inevitably accompanies it.

The Roggen, which was formerly sold under the Shierlinger name, has apparently hit tough times. First, it was repackaged and remarketed under the name of the brewing company rather than of the town, and now that the brewery has been purchased by Paulaner of Munich, it looks as if this innovative beer might well be discontinued altogether. If that happens, the beer world will be poorer for its loss.

HEMPEN ALE

Price: $
Freshness & Durability: *
Availability: ✓ ✓ ✓

The hop belongs to the same botanical family as another popular herb, *Cannabis sativa*, or marijuana. Also of that same family is industrial hemp, which, in addition to having many uses as a fiber, has been widely touted in recent years as a foodstuff. Given those family ties, it is perhaps only natural that hemp beer would eventually be brewed.

Beers spiced with hemp won't make you high, though. Industrial hemp by law contains no more than the most minute trace amounts of THC, and authorities carefully check farmers who grow the crop. So the addition of hemp to a brew does nothing more than flavor the beer, and perhaps give it a little extra marketing cachet.

The flavor of the Hempen Ale belies the suggestion that gimmickry alone was behind the development of the brand. The hemp adds a faint herbal-burlap quality to the light smokiness and fruitiness of the aroma, which smells a lot better than it sounds. In the body, the typically malty, chocolaty, fruity taste of a good brown ale is elevated by the hemp's spicy, grainy flavors, and arguably made a little richer in the process. This beer would be at home beside a plate of roast beef with gravy, a smoked meat on rye or even a lightly spicy cigar.

MACLAY OAT MALT STOUT

Price: $$
Freshness & Durability: ✳ ✳
Availability: ✓ ✓

Most oatmeal stouts employ small amounts of rolled oats in the mash, the same kind you use to make your breakfast oatmeal. (This has inspired more than one wag to remark that oatmeal stout is not just for breakfast any more.) Maclay uses malted oats as a variation on the theme, and does so to its advantage.

Because unmalted oats tend to gum up the mash tun, one-twentieth to one-tenth of the total grist is normally used by brewers wishing to tap the rich, silky character the oats bestow upon a brew. By using malted oats, however, Maclay is able to increase that amount to about one-fifth, which certainly contributes to the stout's highly distinctive character.

Brewed according to a recipe that dates from 1895, the Oat Malt Stout is a smooth and luscious beer. While there are hints of the oats in the creamy, milk-chocolaty and modestly roasty aroma, it is on the palate that the oats truly come into play. This stout positively caresses the tongue in smooth, almost unctuous delight, bringing notes of chocolate and porridge with brown sugar as it goes. Yet for all of its sensuous pleasure, the Oat Malt Stout is a surprisingly light beer, completely suitable as an afternoon pick-me-up or partnered for lunch with a sandwich of deli ham and brown mustard.

The brewing community of France can be divided roughly into two regions. The first, better known among beer aficionados, is called French Flanders. Centered around the city of Lille in the district of Nord-Pas-de-Calais, bordering Belgium, it is famous for several artisanal beer styles, including the bière de garde (see page 134).

The other main brewing region, built around the Alsatian city of Strasbourg near the German border, is the one better known to the average French beer drinker since it is the home of France's two largest brewing companies, the Heineken-owned Fischer/Pêcheur and Kronenbourg. The brewing traditions that prevail in Alsace are largely of Germanic origin. They can be seen and tasted in the popular, commercially oriented lagers of the French bistros and brasseries, beers such as Kronenbourg 1664, La Belle Strasbourgeoisie and Meteor. Recent years have seen new styles emerge, and now Alsace has become known for several interesting variations on the beer theme as well.

While some of these beery innovations, such as the lamentable bière à la tequila and bière au rhum, tequila- and rum-flavored brews, respectively, could correctly be classified as novelties, others are more worthy of consideration. One such variation is the bière au malt à whiskey, or peated malt beer. A not-so-distant cousin of the Franconian rauchbier (see page 164), the peated malt beer is, as one might expect, brewed from barley that has been kilned over peat. The reason the French refer to this kind of malt as "whiskey malt" is that the same sort of barley is used as the raw ingredient for Scottish whiskey.

The creation of a peated malt beer was perhaps a brewing inevitability because the first stage in the creation of Scotch whiskey requires the brewing and fermentation of an unhopped beer (which is then distilled into the whiskey). In fact, given that hop-free beers were not uncommon at around the time that whiskey is said to have been invented, it could well be that Scotland's very first whiskey might simply have been the distillation of an ordinary Scottish ale, which would in turn have been the world's first peated malt beer.

The French are enthusiastic consumers of Scotch whiskey – they regularly rate as the world's top whiskey-buying nation, above both the United Kingdom and the United States – and this fact would explain at least in part the popularity of peated malt beers in that country. The first such brew, Adelscott, made its debut in the early 1980s, and while others such as Kronenbourg's Wel Scotch and Amberley from the Pelforth Brewery of Lille have followed since, none has had the impact of the original.

The French whiskey malt beers tend to be slightly strong (around 6% alcohol), lightly to moderately sweet and malty, and with only nuances of smoke and whiskey character. They make fine companions on a cool fall day and pair deliciously with ragouts and roasted beef with gravy. Not surprisingly, they also partner well with a dram of single malt whiskey, preferably of a Lowland or one of the milder Speyside varieties.

Peated malts are employed elsewhere in the brewing world, although oddly, little of their use is found in Scotland. For the most part, brewers outside France tend to reserve them for richer beer styles such as Scottish or Irish ale or stout. Two very flavorful exceptions to this generalization are the bottle-conditioned Raftman from Unibroue of Chambly, Quebec, an odd but tasty amalgam of the French peated style and a basic Belgian ale, and the stunning Adam from Hair of the Dog Brewing of Portland, Oregon, a rich and complex example of a peated malt barley wine. The Fish Brewing Company of Olympia, Washington, more typically brews an intensely peaty Poseidon's Old Scotch Ale, while Portland Brewing of Oregon offers a slight smokiness from peat in its seasonal Malarkey's Wild Irish Ale.

ADELSCOTT

Price: $$
Freshness & Durability: ✳
Availability: ✓✓

When the Adelschoffen subsidiary of Fischer of Alsace developed Adelscott back in the early 1980s, they boldly trumpeted its unveiling by decreeing it "the greatest innovation in brewing this century." Considering that they did so in a century that was still to see the rebirth of craft brewing in North America and a rekindling of interest in premium beer styles worldwide, Fischer's declaration was perhaps a bit premature and more than a little bombastic. Even so, Adelscott's arrival should still be considered a most welcome brewing development.

Unlike the sometimes intensely phenolic rauchbiers of Germany, Adelscott and its peated malt peers are intended to be much more subtly smoky. The comparison is much like a massive Scotch whiskey from Islay contrasted with a modest Lowland malt, or a rack of ribs smoked over mesquite relative to some simply grilled over charcoal; the key to the peated malt brew is in the understatement of its ingredients.

As the original of the style, Adelscott fits this understated bill quite well. Moderately sweet and welcomingly smooth, it whispers its smokiness and backs up this quiet declaration with a rather surprising and warming 6.6% alcohol. Adelscott is well suited to cooler weather and the foods that go along with it, particularly the Alsatian specialty choucroutte, a sauerkraut-based dish.

PYRAMID TILTED KILT ALE

Price: $
Freshness & Durability: ＊ ＊
Availability: ✓ ✓

Despite its apparent cultural appropriateness, peated malt is rarely if ever used in modern Scotch ales that hail from Scotland. In his style book, *Scotch Ale*, author and brewer Gregory Noonan writes that "only one brewery in memory brewed a beer with a peat 'reek' (the smoky flavor, valued in whiskies)." He then goes on to describe this beer as one of the Maclachlan brewery's ales, available in Edinburgh during the 1960s, and reports that it was at one time the top-selling beer in that city. American and other non-Scottish brewers, however, have not been at all hesitant to make the marriage of malt and style that the Scots have not. One of the frontrunners in this trend was the Pyramid Brewery with its Tilted Kilt Ale.

First brewed in 1996, the Tilted Kilt was originally known as Pyramid Scotch Ale and was introduced as part of the brewery's special Sphinx Series of characterful, draft-only brews. The reception was such, though, that they brought it back the very next year as a bottled specialty and continue to brew it as their winter seasonal. A warming ale with a mellow peatiness, complex, coffee-ish malt character and a faint memory of Islay in the finish, the Tilted Kilt is just the thing for when the cold rains of winter lash Seattle and the rest of the Pacific Northwest and send residents running for comfort.

BEERS BEYOND THE NORM

People place limits on themselves all the time. "I won't see a movie starring so-and-so." "I don't like eating that type of food." "I wouldn't be caught dead wearing this or that designer label." It's all so, well, limiting.

Beer drinkers put limits upon the kinds of beers that they will drink, too. I have encountered British ale imbibers who won't tolerate lagers, German lager lovers who disdain ales, and brewers who eschew anything not brewed according to the Reinheitsgebot. Again, limiting.

I was once one of those drinkers, but then I discovered that the wonder of beer is the vast, almost infinite number of ways in which it can be brewed. And, as a corollary, I soon found that by stepping outside the ordinary, I discovered a vast array of other tastes and experiences. Since then, I have explored many of those paths, left others for a later date, and enjoyed myself thoroughly. These are some of the beers that I have found along the way.

While fruit beers per se are new to North America, flavored beers are not. When the first European settlers arrived in the New World, they had no fields of grain or endless vines of hops with which to brew beer, so they improvised. Spruce beer was an early favorite, and likely as not other brews were flavored with a variety of herbs and sundry fermentable sugars, perhaps including berries and other fruits.

Yet by the time the 20th century came along, flavored beer in North America was but a distant memory. And by the time the dominant beer culture of the 1970s reared its unapologetically male head, beers made to be anything other than light gold, fizzy and gulpable were viewed with unrestrained suspicion. As for fruit beers, well, forget about it.

All that began to change with the arrival of the craft-beer renaissance, although even today, fruit beers are looked upon by many as questionable beverages – suitable for a lady, perhaps, but certainly not for consumption by a real man. Tellingly, while some fruit beers have scored success on a local or regional level – Pyramid Brewing's Apricot Ale in the Pacific Northwest and Kawartha Lakes Brewing's Raspberry Wheat in southern Ontario, for example – the style has yet to achieve more widespread fame.

Yet despite the lingering stigma, fruit-flavored brews have lately become fairly prolific in North America. Inspired by the lambic-based krieks and framboises of Belgium (see page 50), craft brewers across the United States and, to a more limited degree, Canada have taken to the use of fruit and fruit syrups like the proverbial ducks to water.

There are three ways to create a fruit beer. The first and most difficult involves adding fruit to the mash and/or fermenter. This technique is particularly tricky because the brewer must calculate exactly how much fruit flavor and aroma will be lost as the sugars are consumed during fermentation; even a slight miscalculation can result in a beer that is fruity in name only. The second and more common method calls for blending fruit extract or syrup into the finished beer. Here, the calculations are more simple – akin to seasoning a stew or a soup to taste – but still require some degree of vigilance on the part of the brewer. Finally, the simple system favored by some bars and brewpubs takes the final step to the draft tap and calls for the addition of a spoonful or two of berries and syrup to the pint already poured.

Since most brewers want the added fruit to have a distinct flavor and aroma – otherwise, why bother? – the most common beer style used as a base for a fruit beer is a light wheat ale. This combination makes for a wonderful warm-weather beer and a pleasing year-round aperitif. Some of the well-balanced examples of this type include the aforementioned Pyramid Apricot Ale from Seattle, Washington, and Kawartha Lakes Raspberry Wheat from Peterborough, Ontario, as well as the slightly tart Celis Raspberry from Celis Brewing of Austin, Texas.

Not all fruit beers are wheat beers, though. In Michigan, the Kalamazoo Brewing Company brews a firm, sour cherry-ish Bell's Cherry Stout; in Milwaukee, Wisconsin, the Lakefront Brewery takes it to the bottom of the fermenter with its splendid Pumpkin Beer; and in Ontario, the Niagara Falls Brewing Company perfectly flavors a 6% alcohol ale to create its Apple Ale. Partnering these and other richly flavorful fruit beers with fruit desserts makes for a fabulous end to any meal.

Nor are all nonlambic fruit beers brewed in North America. In recent years, the idea of fruit in a beer has spread worldwide, and fine fruity flavors may now be found in Sweden (Östgöta Blåbärs, a tart blueberry lager from Götarsvik Gårdsbryggeri of Glanshammar), England (Apricot and Strawberry from the Samuel Smith–owned Melbourn Bros. brewery of Stamford), the Czech Republic (the banana-flavored lager Banánové Pivo from the Prague brewpub Pivovarský Dům) and France (La Choulette Framboise, a raspberry bière de garde from the Brasserie La Choulette of Hordain).

NEW GLARUS WISCONSIN BELGIAN RED

Price: $$
Freshness & Durability: ✳
Availability: ✓ ✓

When I first visited the New Glarus Brewing Company in 1994, I was introduced to a new beer that, I was told, contained a full pound (450 g) of Wisconsin cherries for every 750 mL (25-oz) bottle. Wisely, brewery co-owner Deborah Carey saved the tasting of the Belgian Red to the last, following their fine Uff-da Bock, Staghorn Oktoberfest märzen and Irish-style Snowshoe Ale.

If you have never tasted a beer to which one pound of cherries has been added during fermentation, it is difficult to understand the intensity of the fruit that greets you both at the nose and on the palate. To the same degree, it would be an error to suggest that this beer is all fruit and no barley. Like all great fruit beers, the Belgian Red treads that careful line between fruit and beer flavors, and does so expertly. It is a balance that separates classic fruit beers from beers that taste nothing like fruit or like nothing but fruit.

In the years following my first visit to New Glarus Brewing, the company has widened its fruit beer portfolio to include an Apple Ale and a Raspberry Tart, both of which, like the Belgian Red, are brewed with real fruit rather than flavorings or concentrates. It is a testament to the brewing ability of Dan Carey, the man behind the beers, that any one of the three could be listed here as a classic example of a fruit beer.

MEXICALI ROGUE

Price: $$
Freshness & Durability: ✳
Availability: ✓✓

From almost the very first day I began cooking for myself, I have been a fan of spicy food. So when I encountered my very first chili pepper beer, I was delighted. Here, finally, I thought, was a way to combine my admiration of two fine foodstuffs: chilies and beer.

Wrong. The problem with that first chili beer, as with so many others, was that it was all chili and no beer. I liked the taste because I like the taste of peppers, but there was not even a nuance of beer flavor to be found. As a chili pepper rush, it was fine; as a beer, it was a dud.

Enter Rogue Ales of Newport, Oregon. With a deft brewing hand, Rogue's brewer, John Maier, unearthed the ideal balance between chipotole peppers and beer, a balance that gave the flavor of the fruit to the body of the brew without masking the inherent qualities of either. Finally, I could have my pepper and drink it, too.

Since my first taste of the moderately peppery, malty Mexicali Rogue, I have discovered numerous occasions that it fits to a tee, such as alongside a kosher dill pickle, with tortilla chips and green salsa or on its own on a patio in the sunshine. Interestingly, though, it doesn't pair that well with spicy food, as the pepper in the dish tends to cancel out the pepper in the beer. Proof, I suppose, that there really is such a thing as too much of a good thing.

SPICED BEERS

To the average German brewer and a great many of the North American beer "purists," the use of anything other than water, hops, malt and yeast in the creation of a beer is tantamount to heresy. I have been told that the use of spice, for example, is a sign of "sloppy brewing," and that any beer that does not conform to the Bavarian purity law, the Reinheitsgebot, is in a word, "crap."

In the German brewing culture, where bottom-fermentation is the rule and cleanliness of both brewery and beer flavor the ultimate achievements, these feelings are understandable. For while it is not at all uncommon for a bock, a märzen or even a top-fermented hefeweizen to be described as spicy, these flavors and aromas arise from the interplay between the malt, hops, yeast and water, not from any added spice. To the German brewer, the addition of spice would undermine this wonderful alchemy and cause the ruin of a fine, traditional brew.

In truth, however, the use of herbs, spices and other flavoring ingredients in beer predates the 1516 Reinheitsgebot by centuries, even millennia. There is evidence that the earliest brewers in Egypt and Sumeria used coriander and other spices in the creation of their beers, and there is conjecture that brewers in the Amazon basin at about the same time were engaged in a similarly spicy sort of brewing. We also know that the Saxons had their wassail bowl filled with liberally seasoned brew, and that since hops were not in widespread use until around 800 AD, other herbs were likely employed prior to that. Placed in that context, all of a sudden a little nutmeg or allspice added to your brew doesn't really seem terribly odd.

The foremost modern practitioners of brewing with spices are the Belgians. From their famed orange peel and coriander spiced white beers (see page 67) to their affection for putting everything from fruit to mint to ginger into their brews, spiced ales abound in the nation known as Het Bierland, or "The Beer country." Some spiced beers are subtly seasoned variations on classic styles, such as the gingery Saison 1900 of Brasserie Lefèbvre from Quenast, while others incorporate generous handfuls of several different spices, like the liberally seasoned lineup of ales from the steam-powered Brasserie à Vapeur of Pipaix.

Elsewhere in Europe, spiced beers do not engender anywhere near the same kind of following, save for a cluster of British brews like the St. Peter's Spiced Ale of the St. Peter's Brewery of Suffolk, goosed with apple and cinnamon, and a handful of others from mostly northern countries. In North America, however, the style has blossomed.

From the lush Bière Extra Forte de Noël of Montreal, Quebec's Cheval Blanc Brewery, seasoned with ginger, cinnamon and coriander, to the zesty Honey Ginger Beer of Golden Prairie Brewing in Chicago, Illinois, spices have proved to be very popular with many of the continent's craft brewers. Often but by no means exclusively used in seasonal beers, there seems to be no end to the variety of herbs and spices that North American brewers are willing to test, including basil (Lemongrass and Basil Wheat Beer of Berkeley, California's Bison Brewing), grains of paradise (Samuel Adams Summer Ale of the national Boston Beer Company) and St. John's wort (Chicory Stout from the Dogfish Head Brewery in Lewes, Delaware).

It is almost impossible to say exactly how best to enjoy a beer brewed with spices, since the right time for a spiced Belgian strong ale will be different from the best occasion for a spiced wheat beer or a seasoned stout. Because they are all so different, perhaps the only generalization is that spiced beers are perfect for when your preconceptions about beer need a little shaking up.

MAUDITE

Price: $
Freshness & Durability: ✳ ✳ ✳
Availability: ✓ ✓ ✓

When Quebec businessman André Dion started Unibroue in 1992, he decided that he would focus his hiring gaze almost exclusively on young people. That way, he figured, none of his employees would come to the company with bad habits. While you can doubt the validity of his thesis, there is no questioning its results: Unibroue is one of the most successful small breweries in Canada today.

Key to this success is a Belgian brewer named Gino Vantieghem. One of the young people Dion hired early on, Vantieghem has crafted a dozen or so fine beers for Unibroue, most of them strong, many of them spiced and almost all of them inspired by Belgian brewing traditions. In addition to the Maudite, Unibroue offers the tripel-ish Eau Bénite ("Holy Water"), a white beer, Blanche de Chambly, named for the town the brewery calls home, and a fruity, 9% alcohol golden ale with the ominous moniker of La Fin du Monde, or "The End of the World."

While Vantieghem will not disclose the spices contained in any of his brews, he will admit to using spice in the making of Maudite, and it certainly shows. The 8% alcohol ale, the name of which translates to "Damned," is a veritable potpourri of a beer, with notes of clove, allspice, cinnamon and other spices. The difficulty, of course, is in figuring out which come from spice additions and which arise through the chemistry of brewing and fermentation. This is not all bad, however, as it offers a happy excuse for opening another bottle of this delicious, dangerously drinkable beer.

LA CHOUFFE

Price: $$$
Freshness & Durability: * * *
Availability: ✓ ✓

Many a commercial brewery was started as a hobby. And since the love of beer and brewing is the single most essential ingredient in the creation of great beer, it comes as no surprise that many of those "hobby businesses" number among the world's great brewing enterprises.

The Brasserie d'Achouffe is a perfect example of one such phenomenon. Opened in 1982 by brothers-in-law Chris Bauweraerts and Pierre Gobron, the little brewery in the Ardennes countryside of Belgium quickly grew to occupy much more than the owners' "hobby time." By 1984, Pierre had left his job to attend to the brewery on a full-time basis, and in 1988, he was joined by Chris. Today, the Brasserie d'Achouffe is internationally one of the best known of Belgium's small breweries, even though finding its beers in the Flemish part of the country can sometimes be quite a challenge. In fact, I once spent a week in Brussels without seeing any evidence of the brewery's products, and subsequently encountered a La Chouffe draft tap in the very first Amsterdam bar I visited.

La Chouffe is the ale upon which the brewery was built. Of 8% alcohol, it is a surprisingly light-tasting and drinkable beer, perhaps because it is brewed from pilsner malt and spiced with the refreshing taste of coriander. While there is some fruitiness to the body, the overall effect is dry and spicy, with some slight hop notes and lingering spice on the finish, which makes it a delicious, strong patio beer and a fine complement to poultry at the table.

In the days before international air travel became the everyday occurrence it is today, misunderstandings concerning the beers of another country were commonplace. For example, a generation of soldiers returning to North America from England after the Second World War fostered the mistaken notion that all Brits enjoyed their beer served warm. The truth was that the English ales were actually being poured at cellar temperature, but relative to the icy-cold lagers the G.I.s were used to drinking, it must have seemed to them very much on the tepid side.

Even if based on a misunderstanding, there was some truth to what the soldiers were claiming. For at one time, the British pub-goer did drink warm or even steaming hot ale. But then again, so did the colonists in the New World.

Around the time of the American Revolution, beer consumption in colonial taverns was in a rather curious state. Inspired perhaps by the variable and sometimes highly questionable quality of the beers of the time, colonists had turned to mixed beer drinks. Often incorporating rum, molasses, spices, eggs or even cream, these frequently potent mixtures went by such curious names as Rumfustian, Syllabub, Whistle Belly Vengeance and, my favorite, Dog's Nose. (Imagine entering a pub and asking the bartender for a Dog's Nose!) While some of these drinks were enjoyed cold or at room temperature, many were served warm or hot, and often heated up in a most ingenious fashion.

Take, for example, the king of all colonial beer drinks, the Beer Flip. Composed primarily of ale and rum or some other spirit, the Flip was also sweetened with sugar, molasses or dried pumpkin and primed with a well-beaten egg or two. Then a red-hot iron poker was thrust into the middle of the mixture and the drink not only turned hot but also foamed and bubbled up over the sides of the mug and onto the table or bar. The patrons loved it, although I strongly suspect that the bartenders most profoundly did not.

Based on the fact that Old World brewing nations like Germany and

Britain still have some popular mixed beer drinks – colabier, or lager mixed with cola, and lager and lime among them – it is a fairly safe bet that mixed beer drinks were common in other lands at the time as well. And since most of the beer culture of the colonies came from England, it is also likely that the Brits of the 18th century were drinking their own Beer Flips, or at least their own variations on the theme. (Although it should also be noted that since British beer drinkers were citizens of a nation that at the time had a much more modern brewing industry and infinitely better supply of ingredients than did the colonists, there was likely less cause to disguise the taste of the ale and correspondingly less interest in beer drinks.)

Like so much of the olden-day beer culture, mulled beer is today on the comeback trail. While I have yet to find anyone willing to admit to a fondness for Flip, I have with increasing frequency found myself encountering beer aficionados who claim a special affection for hot brews. Perhaps inspired by the ground-breaking Glühkriek of Liefmans, these individuals have warmed up everything from strong English ales to Trappist beers, often in response to a nagging cold or flu.

Personally, I don't feel the need to wait until I'm ill to heat up a beer; any cold winter's eve will do. Faced with the irrationality of an icy-cold brew when the snow is blowing and the temperature is so low the thermometer threatens to crack, I find that a cup of steaming hot beer can be just the thing. Although in deference to the brewer's intent, I do tend to stick to those that are intended to be consumed hot.

LIEFMANS GLÜHKRIEK

Price: $$$
Freshness & Durability: ✳ ✳
Availability: ✓ ✓

You have to wonder just what it was that inspired Liefmans in the mid-1990s to reach back through time and grab the idea of a beer that was meant to be mulled before consumption. From a small independent brewery in the countryside, where the most unusual brewing ideas in Belgium are normally hatched, it would be an extraordinary development. From a brewery owned by the national brewing company, Riva, it rates as a once-in-a-blue-moon phenomenon.

Regardless of why it happened, though, beer aficionados should be thankful. For by developing the first mulling beer that most people have seen, Liefmans not only gave the world another very fine, very satisfying ale, they also opened up the marketplace to the idea of hot beer.

Glüh is a German prefix meaning "to glow," and attached to -*wein*, it forms the word used to describe mulled wine. Bilingually attached to the Flemish word *kriek*, it describes this fine spiced cherry beer that indeed does have the ability to make a body glow, figuratively at least. The aroma is quite fruity with background cinnamon notes, while the body is big with sour cherry on the front but gentle with spice and warming 6% alcohol on the finish. Whether skiing the Swiss Alps in January or weathering the winter on Belgium's northern coast, you will find this to be the perfect beer to drink nice and hot at the end of the day.

QUELQUE CHOSE

Price: $$
Freshness & Durability: ✳ ✳
Availability: ✓ ✓

Living a four-hour drive from the Quebec border, I received word of Unibroue's new mulling beer first as rumor, then as more reliable gossip, and finally as indisputable fact. The next time I encountered it was in a café in Montreal's artistic Plateau Mont Royal neighborhood on a lousy January afternoon after a soggy, snowy hike up rue St-Laurent.

My romantic notions of a steaming kettle of Quelque Chose sitting on the stove in the back were immediately dashed when I saw the bartender crack open a bottle, pour it into a cup and slip it into the microwave for heating. But when I was served my mug of close-to-boiling beer, I realized that this was not about romantic notions but about great beer.

Inspired by the Liefmans Glühkriek, the Quelque Chose is similarly styled but a much bigger beer in virtually every way. The merely assertive cherry of the Belgian original is a massive wallop of fruit in the Quebec challenger, the spice is similarly increased in vigor, and the alcohol is bumped two percentage points to 8%. How you respond to the Liefmans or the Quelque Chose will depend on whether you like your beers mild and more reserved or big and potent. While I enjoy both, I particularly like the wake-up call my palate gets from the bigger beer, and the relaxation my mind draws from the higher strength.

FESTIVAL AND SEASONAL BEERS

Examples of the brewer's vital role in major festivals and ceremonies abound in both modern and ancient history. In her book, *The Rituals of Dinner*, Margaret Visser speaks of the Saxons' wassail bowl, which was brought out on occasions of great honor filled with a distinctive, prepared mulled ale. Similarly, as noted by beer historian Gregg Smith in his book *Beer*, the ancient Babylonians brewed unique beers as offerings to different goddesses during their feast days, and the word *bridal* may be a contraction of "bride ale," a beer brewed by the bride's family for the wedding celebration.

Plainly put, long before Champagne became the liquid of choice for toasting grand occasions, our ancestors used beer for all sorts of celebrations – not just any beer, mind, but beer that was specifically and uniquely brewed for that given feast day, goddess ceremony or other important event. This festive beer tradition, dormant and forgotten for much of the 20th century, has been recently and gloriously revived by today's new generation of brewers. With one eye directed to the pages of brewing history and the other often admittedly trained on the promotional potential of an out-of-the-ordinary, one-off brew, many modern breweries have taken to celebrating special dates and events with equally special beers. In some cases, these brews have even become much-anticipated annual traditions.

There are no stylistic constraints on these festive or seasonal beers, although they are most often of greater strength and more intense character than a brewery's normal fare. Frequently, they are created after a brewery owner or manager instructs the brewer to devise something extraordinary and damn the costs. The resulting beers often end up representing the best a brewer has to offer.

Neither are there national limitations on the brewing of seasonal beers. Unlike certain ales that can be said to be specifically of a British or Belgian style, or lagers that are Czech or German in nature, no one nation can claim dominion over the desire to celebrate. So seasonal and festive beers come not only in all styles but also from all corners of the globe.

Figuring very strongly in the international festive beer mix are hugely flavorful and potent brews, be they top-fermented like the Bush de Noël from the Pipaix, Belgium, brewer Dubuisson or lager-brewed like the Noche Buena from the national brewery Femsa Cerveza of Mexico. Also playing a prominent role in worldwide celebrations are spiced brews such Our Special Ale, a Christmas beer brewed to a different recipe each year, from Anchor Brewing in San Francisco, California, and Ale Bopp, a nutmeg and cinnamon spiced beer from the Hopback Brewery in Salisbury, England.

In the years since the start of the craft-brewing renaissance, seasonal beers have become particularly popular in the United States. Largely centered around Christmas, they are brewed to be big and bold, highly hoppy and intensely alcoholic. One well-known and long-standing seasonal from the East is the Hampshire Special Ale, a big, malty, dry-finishing winter brew from Geary Brewing of Portland, Maine. The Pacific Northwest and northern California offer a host of winter seasonals, including the cinnamon and mocha-ish Jubelale of Bend, Oregon's Deschutes Brewery, the herbal Bert Grant's Winter Ale from Yakima Brewing in Yakima, Washington, and the big, spicy Winter Solstice Select Ale from Anderson Valley Brewing in Booneville, California.

With so many breweries across North America brewing celebratory beers, though, finding good festive and seasonal brews in any given area is often as simple as making a trip to the local brewpub, ale house or beer store and seeing what's available. And as for the best time to enjoy them, that much is obvious: any celebration!

Samuel Smith Winter Welcome

Price: $$
Freshness & Durability: ✳ ✳
Availability: ✓ ✓ ✓

Dating from 1758, the Samuel Smith Brewery of Tadcaster, Yorkshire, is not only the oldest brewery in England, it is also one of the most ardently traditional. In the typical Yorkshire fashion, the brewery still employs the "Yorkshire square" method of fermentation, the complicated, two-level system required for the circulation of the typically stubborn Yorkshire yeasts. Other northern brewers also use the traditional system, but only Samuel Smith can lay claim to the last remaining Yorkshire squares made of stone in the land.

In this age of brewery concentration, Samuel Smith is in its fifth generation of family ownership. Horse-drawn drays to service the brewery and the wooden barrels for the Smith cask ales are still used.

Then, of course, there are the beers. In addition to revivalist Imperial and oatmeal stouts, one of the very few commendable English lagers and fine pale and India pale ales, Samuel Smith offers a Christmas seasonal very much in the celebratory tradition of centuries past. The label, though of different design each year, is always festive and seems to present the ale as a "thank-you" to loyal Smith customers. To my palate, the beer is also altered slightly each year, but that may be due more to changes in supplies than intent. It is a fine strong (6% alcohol) ale with full body, restrained fruitiness, the nuttiness typical of the brewery's ales and a lightly sherry-ish finish. A grand beer for a celebration.

BOSKEUN

Price: $$$
Freshness & Durability: ✳ ✳ ✳
Availability: ✓

Easter may not be the season most associated with beer, but neither is De Dolle Brouwers exactly the most typical of breweries. And when a company called "The Mad Brewers" wants to brew a special Easter beer, complete with a picture of a cute beer-drinking bunny on the label, the best thing to do is let them go ahead and do it – then enjoy the results.

The story behind De Dolle Brouwers is the kind of a tale that makes otherwise sane, normal individuals want to leap straight into the beer business. Faced with the prospect that their town might be without a brewery once the local one had closed down, three beer-loving brothers, backed by their mother, bought the old business in 1980 and resurrected it as a new brewing company. At first it was a weekend-only opera-tion, mostly just a hobby for the former home-brewers, but eventually word spread of their highly individualistic beers and success soon followed. Their beer is now sold not only in Belgium but also in four export markets, including the United States.

Besides the gingery, honey-ish Boskeun, which is fittingly wonderful alongside hot cross buns, De Dolle Brouwers brews two other seasonals. For the summer they offer a golden, delicately strong Oeral, and in winter they provide the sweet, complex, 8% alcohol Stille Nacht, meaning "Silent Night."

THE PREMIUM BEER DRINKER'S QUICK GUIDE

Because sometimes you have to make your beer buying decisions more quickly than others, the Quick Guide provides an easy reference to all of the beer styles explored in this book, complete with serving suggestions and short lists of North American and international examples.

And to make things even easier, I have also compiled several brief-and-basic "beer-at-glance" charts. These illustrated references offer food and beer pairing suggestions for brunch, barbecue, dessert and more and recommend eight beers for each of the four seasons.

LAMBIC AND GUEUZE

Tart, sometimes acidic wheat beers; refreshing and invigorating

International Examples: Cantillon Gueuze, Hanssens Oude Gueuze, Drie
Fonteinen Gueuze

North American Examples: Rare

FRUIT LAMBIC

Fruit-flavored beers often with tart characters; perfect aperitifs

International Examples: Boon Mariage Parfait Kriek, Cantillon Rose de
Gambrinus, Cantillon St. Lamvinus

North American Examples: Rare

FLEMISH RED AND BROWN ALE

Tart fruity brown and red ales of Belgium; good with beef and game dishes

International Examples: Rodenbach Grand Cru, Liefmans Goudenband,
Duchesse de Bourgogne

North American Examples: Rare

HEFEWEIZEN

Refreshingly spicy, sometimes banana-y, bottle-conditioned wheat beers

International Examples: Schneider Weisse, Weihenstephaner Hefeweissbier,
Hitachino Nest Hefeweizen

North American Examples: Tabernass Weiss, DeGroen's Weizen, Agassiz
Harvest Haze Hefeweizen

WHITE BEER

Brewed with orange peel and coriander; ideal for brunch and summer days

International Examples: Hoegaarden White, Blanche de Bruges, Blanche des
Honnelles

North American Examples: Celis White, Blanche de Chambly, Cheval Blanc
Bière Blanche Originale

WEIZENBOCK

Paradoxically warming and refreshing wheat beers; perfect with a plate of sausage and sauerkraut

International Examples: Schneider Aventinus, Erdinger Pikantus, Maisel Weizenbock

North American Examples: DeGroen's Weizenbock, Victory Moonglow Weizenbock

NORTH AMERICAN PALE ALE

Bitter and fruity ales for casual enjoyment or with a meal

International Examples: Rare

North American Examples: Sierra Nevada Pale Ale, St. Ambroise Pale Ale, Three Floyds Alpha King

INDIA PALE ALE

Pale ales with greater intensity and higher alcohol; good spicy-food beers

International Examples: Rare in their true, historic form

North American Examples: Anchor Liberty Ale, Brooklyn East IPA, Storm Hurricane IPA

BOCK

Moderately strong lagers for greeting the spring; delicious with pork dishes

International Examples: Einbecker Ur-Bock, Aass Bock, Ayinger Maibock, Schlenkerla UrBock

North American Examples: New Glarus Uff-da Bock, Saxer Bock, Creemore Springs Ur-Bock

DOPPELBOCK

Strong, malty and full-bodied lagers; ideal with chocolate cake

International Examples: Paulaner Salvator, Spaten Optimator, Ayinger
Celebrator, Moretti La Rossa

North American Examples: Samuel Adams Double Bock, Stoudt Honey Double
Mai-Bock, Brick Bock

EISBOCK

Very strong bocks with concentrated flavor and alcohol; late-night beers

International Examples: Reichelbräu Eisbock Bayrisch G'frorns (vintage only)

North American Examples: Niagara Falls Eisbock, Vancouver Island
Hermannator

CASK-CONDITIONED BEST BITTER

Sociable ales with moderate hoppiness and balanced fruit

International Examples: Marstons Pedigree, Batemans XXXB, many others

North American Examples: Sporadically available from select small breweries
and brewpubs

CASK-CONDITIONED STRONG ALE

Malty and fulfilling ale for meals or after dinner

International Examples: King & Barnes Festive Ale, Fuller's ESB,
Badger Tanglefoot

North American Examples: Sporadically available from select small breweries
and brewpubs

CASK-FLAVORED ALES

Strong cask flavors figure in these complex, late-night tipples

International Examples: Rare

North American Examples: Samuel Adams Triple Bock, Goose Island Bourbon
County Stout

SCOTCH ALE

Intensely malty strong ales; very fine dessert beers or companions to cheese

International Examples: McEwan's Scotch Ale, Douglas/Gordon Highland Scotch Ale, McChouffe

North American Examples: Samuel Adams Scotch Ale, Road Dog Ale, McAuslan Scotch Ale

IMPERIAL STOUT

Extremely strong, rich, fulfilling stouts; perfect for late night

International Examples: Samuel Smith Imperial Stout, Courage Imperial Russian Stout (vintage only), Sinebrychoff Porter

North American Examples: Rasputin Imperial Russian Stout, Grant's Imperial Stout, Wellington County Imperial Stout

STRONG STOUT AND PORTER

Strong, sweet but relatively light and oddly refreshing ales; good cigar beers

International Examples: (Strong Porter) Saku Porter, Okocim Porter, Zywiec Porter

North American Examples: (Strong Stout) Dragon Stout, Royal Lion Stout, Banks Ebony

ABBEY-STYLE ALE

Malt-dominated ales that are good with rich stews or desserts

International Examples: Floreffe Dubbel, Affligem Dubbel, Maredsous 8°

North American Examples: Ommegang Belgian-Style Abbey Ale, New Belgium Abbey, Seigneuriale

BIÈRE DE GARDE AND SAISON

Strong but refreshing "farmhouse" ales; excellent with cheese

International Examples: (bière de garde) Trois Monts, Jenlain, (saison) Saison
 Dupont, Saison de Silly

North American Examples: Rare

STRONG GOLDEN ALE

Dry, spritzy, refreshing and surprisingly strong ales; wonderful as aperitifs

International Examples: Duvel, Lucifer, Sloeber, Delerium Tremens

North American Examples: Don de Dieu, Hennepin, Pranqster, Wentzel's
 Winter Warmer

TRIPEL

Strong golden ales with sweet complexity; after-dinner beers or restoratives

International Examples: Westmalle Tripel, Brugs Tripel, Affligem Tripel

North American Examples: Eau Bénite, Celis Grand Cru, New Belgium Tripel
 Belgian-Style Ale

BARLEY WINE

Intensely flavorful, high-alcohol brews; perfect as a nightcap

International Examples: Young's Old Nick, Fuller's Golden Pride, Gibbs Mew
 the Bishop's Tipple

North American Examples: Anchor Old Foghorn, Sierra Nevada Bigfoot,
 Rogue Old Crustacean

ENGLISH OLD ALE

Round, well-developed and fruity ales for quiet contemplation at the end
 of the day

International Examples: J.W. Lee's Harvest Ale, Thomas Hardy's Ale,
 Gale's Prize Old Ale

North American Examples: Hibernation Ale, Wizard's Winter Ale, Third
 Coast Old Ale

TRAPPIST ALE

Complex, malty, strong ales; good with chocolate, desserts or as digestifs

International Examples: Rochefort, Westmalle, Chimay, La Trappe, Westvleteren, Orval

North American Examples: None exist

RAUCHBIER AND OTHER SMOKED MALT BEERS

Moderately to highly smoky beers that are right at home beside the barbecue

International Examples: Aecht Schlenkerla Märzen, Kaiserdom Rauchbier, Spezial Lagerbier

*North American Examples:*Alaskan Smoked Porter, Rogue Smoke, DeGroen's Rauchbock

STRANGE GRAINS

Often spicy-tasting beers accented by unusual grains; flavor varies according to style

International Examples: Thurn und Taxis Roggen (rye), Maclay Oat Malt Stout, Brasserie Silenrieux Sara (buckwheat)

North American Examples: Redhook Rye, St. Ambroise Oatmeal Stout, Hempen Ale

PEATED MALT BEER

Mildly smoky, malty beers; North American examples are more intense

International Examples: Adelscott, Wel Scotch, Amberley

North American Examples: Raftman, Hair of the Dog Adam, Poseidon's Old Scotch Ale, Pyramid Tilted Kilt Ale

Fruit Beers

Fruit-flavored beers varying greatly in degree and intensity of fruit flavor

International Examples: Östgöta Blåbärs, Melbourn Bros. Apricot, La
Choulette Framboise

North American Examples: New Glarus Wisconsin Belgian Red, Mexicali
Rogue, Niagara Falls Apple Ale

Spiced Beers

Beers seasoned with various spices; style and intensity of seasoning varies

International Examples: La Chouffe, Saison 1900, St. Peter's Spiced Ale

North American Examples: Maudite, Golden Prairie Honey Ginger Beer,
Dogfish Head Chicory Stout

Mulling Beers

Hot, spiced ales to warm body and soul on a cold winter's day

International Examples: Liefmans Glükriek

North American Examples: Quelque Chose

Festive and Seasonal Beers

A diverse category of ales and lagers styled for celebration

International Examples: Samuel Smith Winter Welcome, De Dolle Brouwers
Boskeun, Bush de Noël

North American Examples: Anchor Our Special Ale, Geary Hampshire Special
Ale, Bert Grant's Winter Ale

Beer at the Table

Aperitif

**Boon Mariage
Parfait Kriek
(page 52)**

**Cantillon Rosé
de Gambrinus
(page 53)**

**Batemans xxxb
(page 102)**

**Duvel
(page 140)**

Brunch

**Schneider Weiss
(page 64)**

**Weihenstephaner
Hefeweissbier
(page 66)**

**Hoegaarden
(page 69)**

**Celis White
(page 70)**

Barbecue

**Aventius
(page 73)**

**Aecht Schenkerla
Rauchbier
(page 166)**

**Alaskan Smoked
Porter
(page 167)**

**Adelscott
(page 176)**

Spicy Foods

**Sierra Nevada
Pale Ale
(page 78)**

**St. Ambroise Pale
Ale
(page 79)**

**Anchor Liberty
Ale
(page 82)**

**Brooklyn East
India Pale Ale
(page 83)**

HEARTY FARE

**King & Barnes
Festive Ale
(page 106)**

**Fuller's ESB
(page 107)**

**Douglas/Gordon
Scotch Ale
(page 116)**

**Traquair House
Ale
(page 117)**

DESSERT

**Salvator
(page 93)**

**Affligem Dubbel
(page 131)**

**Old Foghorn
(page 148)**

**New Glarus Wisconsin
Belgian Red
(page 182)**

CHOCOLATE

**Liefmans
Goudenband
(page 59)**

**Samuel Smith
Imperial Stout
(page 120)**

**Floreffe Dubbel
(page 130)**

**Rochefort 8°
(page 160)**

WITH A CIGAR

**Samuel Adams
Tripel Bock
(page 111)**

**North Coast
Rasputin Imperial
Russian Stout
(page 121)**

**Dragon Stout
(page 125)**

**Hempen Ale
(page 172)**

Eight Beers for Each Season

Spring

Hanssens Oude Gueuze (page 49)

Liefmans Goudenband (page 59)

Anchor Liberty Ale (page 82)

Einbecker Ur-Bock (page 88)

Aass Bock (page 89)

Mexicali Rogue (page 183)

La Chouffe (page 187)

Boskeun (page 197)

Summer

Cantillion Rosé de Gambrinus (page 53)

Rodenbach Grand Cru (page 58)

Celis White (page 70)

Aventinus (page 73)

Saku Porter (page 126)

Saison Dupont (page 137)

Westmalle Triple (page 143)

Hempen Ale (page 172)

FALL

**Niagara Falls
Eisbock
(page 97)**

**Fuller's ESB
(page 107)**

**Trois Monts
(page 136)**

**J.W. Lee's
Harvest Ale
(page 154)**

**Orval
(page 158)**

**Aecht Schlenkerla
Rauchbier
(page 166)**

**Adelscott
(page 176)**

**Maudite
(page 186)**

WINTER

**Douglas/Gordon
Scotch Ale
(page 116)**

**North Coast
Rasputin Imperial
Russian Stout
(page 121)**

**Bigfoot
(page 149)**

**Rochefort 8°
(page 160)**

**La Trappe
Quadrupel
(page 161)**

**Liefmans
Glühkriek
(page 191)**

**Quelque Chose
(page 192)**

**Samuel Smith
Winter Welcome
(page 196)**

WHERE THE WILD YEASTS ARE

Lambic and Gueuze

Cantillon Gueuze
Brasserie Cantillon
Rue Gheude straat 56
1070 Brussels
Belgium
phone: 02 521 49 28

Hanssens Oude Gueuze
Hanssens Artisanaal BVBA
Vroenenbosstraat 15
1653 Dworp
Belgium
phone: 02 380 31 33

Fruit Lambic

Boon Mariage Parfait Kriek
Brouwerij Frank Boon
Fonteinstraat 65
1502 Lembeek
Belgium
phone: 02 356 66 44

Cantillon Rosé de Gambrinus
Brasserie Cantillon
Rue Gheude straat 56
1070 Brussels
Belgium
phone: 02 521 49 28

Cantillon St. Lamvinus
Brasserie Cantillon
Rue Gheude straat 56
1070 Brussels
Belgium
phone: 02 521 49 28

Flemish Red and Brown Ales

Rodenbach Grand Cru
Brouwerij Rodenbach
Spanjestraat 133
8800 Roeselare
Belgium
phone: 051 22 34 00

Liefmans Goudenband
Brouwerij Liefmans
Aalststraat 200
9700 Oudenaarde
Belgium
phone: 055 31 13 92

WHY NOT WHEAT?

Hefeweizen

Schneider Weisse
Privatbrauerei G. Schneider
& Sohn
1–5 Emil Ott Strasse
8420 Kelheim, Bavaria
Germany
phone: 09441 7050

Weihenstephaner Hefeweissbier
Bayerische Staatsbrauerei
Weihenstephaner
Postfach 11 55
D-85311 Freising
Germany
phone: 08161 5360

White Beer

Hoegaarden
Brouwerij de Kluis
Stoopkenstraat 46
3320 Hoegaarden
Belgium
phone: 016 76 76 76

Celis White
Celis Brewery
2431 Forbes Drive
Austin, Texas 78754
United States
phone: 512 835 0884

Weizenbock

Aventinus
Privatbrauerei G. Schneider
& Sohn
1–5 Emil Ott Strasse
8420 Kelheim, Bavaria
Germany
phone: 09441 7050

HOPS GOOD, MORE HOPS BETTER

North American Pale Ale

Sierra Nevada Pale Ale
Sierra Nevada Brewing Company
1075 East 20th Street
Chico, California 95928
United States
phone: 916 893 3520

St. Ambroise Pale Ale
Brasserie McAuslan Brewery
4850 St-Ambroise
Bureau 100
Montreal, Quebec H4C 3N8
Canada
phone: 514 939 3060

India Pale Ale

Anchor Liberty Ale
Anchor Brewing Company
1705 Mariposa Street
San Francisco, California 94107
United States
phone: 415 863 8350

Brooklyn East India Pale Ale
Brooklyn Brewery
79 North 11th Street
Brooklyn, New York 11211
United States
phone: 718 486 7422

BOCK TO BASICS

Bock
Einbecker Ur-Bock
Einbecker Brauhaus
4 Papen Strasse
D-37574 Einbeck, Lower Saxony
Germany
phone: 05561 7970

Aass Bock
Aass Bryggeri
10 Ole Steensgt
3015 Drammen
Norway
phone: 32 26 60 00

Doppelbock
Salvator
Paulaner
75 Hoch Strasse
D-81541 Munich 95
Germany
phone: 089 480050

Celebrator
Brauerei Aying
Zornedinger Strasse 1
D-85653 Aying
Germany
phone: 08095 880

Eisbock
Niagara Falls Eisbock
Niagara Falls Brewing Company
6863 Lundy's Lane
Niagara Falls, Ontario L2G 1V7
Canada
phone: 905 356 2739

FROM THE WOOD

Cask-Conditioned Best Bitter
Batemans XXXB
George Bateman & Son Ltd.
Salem Bridge Brewery
Wainfleet, Lincolnshire
PE24 4JE
England
phone: 01754 880317

Marston's Pedigree
Marston Thompson And
Evershed Plc
Shobnall Road
Burton upon Trent, Stafforshire
DE14 2BW
England
phone: 01283 531131

Cask-Conditioned Strong Ale
King & Barnes Festive Ale
King & Barnes Ltd.
The Horsham Brewery
18 Bishopric
Horsham, West Sussex
RH12 1QP
England
phone: 01403 270470

Fuller's ESB
Fuller Smith & Turner PLC
Griffin Brewery
Chiswick Lane South
Chiswick, London W4 2QB
England
phone: 0181 996 2000

Cask-Flavored Ales
Samuel Adams Triple Bock
Boston Beer Company
30 Germania Street
Boston, Massachussets 02130
United States
phone: 617 522 9080

DON'T BE AFRAID OF THE DARK

Scotch Ale
Douglas Scotch Ale/Gordon
Highland Scotch Ale
John Martin
Rue du Cerf 191
1332 Genval
Belgium
phone: 02 655 62 33

Traquair House Ale
Traquair House Brewery
Traquair Estate
Innerleithen, Peeblesshire
EH44 6PW
Scotland
phone: 01896 830232

Imperial Stout
Samuel Smith Imperial Stout
Samuel Smith Old Brewery
(Tadcaster)
High Street
Tadcaster, North Yorkshire
LS24 9SB
England
phone: 01937 832225

North Coast Rasputin Imperial
Russian Stout
North Coast Brewing Company
455 North Main Street
Fort Bragg, California 95437
United States
phone: 707 964 2739

Strong Stout and Porter
Dragon Stout
Desnoes & Geddes
214 Spanish Town Road
P.O. Box 190
Kingston 11
Jamaica
phone: 876 923 9291

Saku Porter
Saku Brewery
EE 3400
Harju Maakond
Saku, Estonia
phone: 372 6508 400

Abbey-Style Ale
Floreffe Dubbel
Brasserie Lefebvre
Rue de Croly 52
1430 Quenast
Belgium
phone: 067 67 07 66

Affligem Dubbel
Brouwerij de Smedt
Ringlaan 18
1745 Opwijk
Belgium
phone: 052 35 99 11

DEVILS IN DISGUISE

Bière de Garde and Saison
Trois Monts
Brasserie de St-Sylvestre
141 rue de la Chapelle
59114 St-Sylvestre-Cappel
Steenvoorde
France
phone: 03 28 40 15 49

Saison Dupont
Brasserie Dupont
Rue Basse 5
7904 Tourpes-Leuze
Belgium
phone: 069 67 10 66

Strong Golden Ale
Duvel
Brouwerij Moortgat
Breendonkdorp 58
2870 Breendonk-Puurs
Belgium
phone: 03 886 71 21

Tripel
Westmalle Tripel
Abdij der Trappisten
Antwerpsesteenweg 496
2390 Westmalle
Belgium
phone: 03 312 92 00

BEERS FOR THE CELLAR

Barley Wine
Old Foghorn
Anchor Brewing Company
1705 Mariposa Street
San Francisco, California 94107
United States
phone: 415 863 8350

Bigfoot
Sierra Nevada Brewing Company
1075 East 20th Street
Chico, California 95928
United States
phone: 916 893 3520

Old Crustacean
Rogue Ales
2320 OSU Drive
Newport, Oregon 97365
United States
phone: 541 867 3660

English Old Ale
J.W. Lee's Harvest Ale
J.W. Lees And Company
(Brewers) Ltd
Middleton Junction
Manchester M24 2AX
Greengate Brewery
England
phone: 0161 643 2487

Thomas Hardy's Ale
Thomas Hardy Brewing Ltd.
Weymouth Avenue
Dorchester, Dorset DT1 1QT
England
phone: 01305 251251

Trappist Ale
Brasserie d'Orval S.A.
Abbaye Notre-Dame d'Orval
6823 Villers-devant-Orval
Belgium
phone: 061 31 12 61

Rochefort 8°
Abbaye Notre-Dame de Saint-Rémy
Rue de l'Abbaye 8
5580 Rochefort
Belgium
phone: 084 21 31 81

La Trappe Quadrupel
Brouwerij de Schaapskooi
Trappistenabdij OLV van Koningshoeven
Eindhovenseweg 3
5056 RP Berkel-Enschot
Netherlands
phone: 013 535 8147

NOT YOUR AVERAGE BREW

Rauchbier and Other Smoked Malt Beers
Aecht Schlenkerla Märzen
Brauerei Heller-Trum
6 Dominikaner Strasse
D-96049 Bamberg
Germany
phone: 0951 56060

Alaskan Smoked Porter
Alaskan Brewing & Bottling
Company
5429 Shaune Drive
Juneau, Alaska 99801-9540
United States
phone: 907 780 5866

Strange Grains
Thurn und Taxis Roggen
Fürstliche Brauerei Thurn
und Taxis
14 Haupt Strasse
D-84069 Schierling, Bavaria
Germany
phone: 09451 3012

Hempen Ale
Frederick Brewing Company
4607 Wedgewood Boulevard
Frederick, Maryland 21703
United States
phone: 301 694 7899

Maclay Oat Malt Stout
Maclay Group Ltd.
Thistle Brewery
Alloa, Clackmannanshire
FK10 1ED
Scotland
phone: 01259 723387

Peated Malt Beer
Adelscott
Brasseries Fischer & Adelshoffen
9 Route de Bischwiller
BP 48
67301 Schiltigheim
France
phone: 03 88 33 82 00

Pyramid Scotch Ale
Pyramid Breweries Inc.
91 S. Royal Brougham Way
Seattle, Washington 98134
United States
phone: 206 682 8322

BEERS BEYOND THE NORM

Fruit Beers
New Glarus Wisconsin
Belgian Red
New Glarus Brewing Company
County Road West, Hwy. 69
P.O. Box 328
New Glarus, Wisconsin
53574-0328
United States
phone: 608 527 5850

Mexicali Rogue
Rogue Ales
2320 OSU Drive
Newport, Oregon 97365
United States
phone: 541 867 3660

Spiced Beers
Maudite
Unibroue
80 Des Carrières
Chambly, Québec J3L 2H6
Canada
phone: 450 658 7658

La Chouffe
Brasserie d'Achouffe
Route du Village 32
6666 Achouffe-Wibrin
Belgium
phone: 061 28 81 47

Mulling Beers
Liefmans Glühkriek
Huisbrouwerij Liefmans
Aalststraat 200
9700 Oudenaarde
Belgium
phone: 055 31 13 92

Quelque Chose
Unibroue
80 Des Carrières
Chambly, Québec J3L 2H6
Canada
phone: 450 658 7658

Festival and Seasonal Beers
Samuel Smith Winter Welcome
Samuel Smith Old Brewery
(Tadcaster)
High Street
Tadcaster, North Yorkshire
LS24 9SB
England
phone: 01937 832225

Boskeun
De Dolle Brouwers
Roeselarestraat 12b
8600 Esen-Diksmuide
Belgium
phone: 051 50 27 81